Light Theology & Heavy Cream

The Culinary Adventures
of Pietro & Madeleine

Robert Farrar Capon

COWLEY PUBLICATIONS
Cambridge, Massachusetts

Published in the United States of America by Cowley Publications, a division of the Society of Saint John the Evangelist. No portion of this book may be reproduced, stored in or introduced into a retrieval system, or transmitted, in any form or by any means—including photocopying—without the prior written permission of Cowley Publications, except in the case of brief quotations embedded in critical articles and reviews.

Library of Congress Cataloging-in-Publication Data
Capon, Robert Farrar.
 Light theology & heavy cream : the culinary adventures of Pietro & Madeleine / Robert Farrar Capon.
  p. cm.
 Includes bibliographical references and index.
 ISBN 1-56101-266-1 (pbk. : alk. paper) 1. Theology.
2. Table—Religious aspects—Christianity. I. Title: Light theology and heavy cream. II. Title.
 BR115.N87C37 2004
 242—dc22   2004018753

This book was printed in Canada on acid-free paper.

Cover Design: Jennifer Hopcroft
Cover Art: Doug Compton

Cowley Publications
4 Brattle Street
Cambridge, Massachusetts 02138
800-225-1534 • www.cowley.org

Contents

Introduction: A Word from the Stars of This Production   *v*

1   Fast Shuffle   *1*

2   Fortune Smiles   *5*

3   Hands On   *11*

4   Creativity   *17*

5   No Job at All   *21*

6   Simple Dictation   *27*

7   Unlocking the Mystery of Menus   *31*

8   Mystery Train   *35*

9   The Secret Cream Club   *39*

10   Cheeseburger, Cheeseburger   *43*

11   Ax Me No Sinners   *47*

12   Resurrecting Fannie Farmer   *51*

13   The Great Zucchini   *55*

14   From the Woodshed   *59*

15   Held in Contempt   *65*

16   Angelique Bedeviled   *69*

17   Angelique Diabolique   *73*

18   Mr. Ewing Goes to Washington   *77*

19   Thirty-two Pounds of Pork   *81*

20   Banishing the Blues With a Red Sauce   *85*

21   The Short and Long of It   *89*

22   Carlo the Crass   *93*

23   Ockham's Razor   *97*

24   Dinner in the Diner   *101*

25   Spirituality   *105*

26   The Final Hampton   *109*

A Word from the Stars of this Production

The book before you can best be described as culinary and theological snack food—a literary meal consisting entirely of *hors d'oeuvre*. While it is not without nutritive value on the count of either cooking or thinking, it is principally intended as a lark. Our personae as Pietro and Madeleine—the protagonists, or better said, the antagonists in this book—are extrapolations of the idiosyncrasies of the author and his wife, Valerie. He stumbled on the name *Madeleine* for her early in their marriage when he took to complimenting her breakfast efforts by saying, inexplicably, "Good coffee, Madeleine." The name *Pietro* was inspired by some occasional pieces that John Leonard wrote for The *New York Times*—pieces in which a fictitious critic named Dmitri served as a mouthpiece for Leonard's own opinions. Dmitri having been used up or burned out, Pietro was created to fill his shoes. We are pleased to have been presented as (mostly) delightful characters, though we are not without a hankering, at some future date, to give the author a dose of his own medicine.

Still, our fondness for him outpaces our objections. For a writer so deeply in love with theology and cookery, he has the happy faculty of being not only able but eager to offend the powers that be in both fields. He gleefully berates the church for being more preoccupied with stringencies of religion than with the Good News of forgiveness, and he twists the tails of diet-mongers and food snobs with equal abandon. There is no king in either country whose lack of clothes he does not stigmatize. Therefore as he lurks behind our masks in this potpourri of fulminations, bickering, and badinage, we become a fun-house mirror held up to his own style. If he has seldom been content to stay on one subject, here he flits wildly between the dozens of old films in the multiplex of his mind. If he has always been perfectly substantial and perfectly silly at the same time, here he propels himself faster and farther in both directions.

For the record, all the pieces in this book were composed between 1978 and 1988. He has made no effort to update references to the clergy, politicians, or food prices of that period: Jim Bakker, Gary Hart, Ronald Reagan, and a three-star restaurant that charged a mere sixty dollars for a dinner for two (wine and tips included) have all been left as they were to exasperate or titillate you anew—or to make you pine for the days when the dollar actually worked for its living. If you have enjoyed the author's light touch in the rest of his *oeuvre*, you will continue to enjoy it here. On the other hand, if you have deemed his work mere popularizing, you will no doubt relegate this book to bathroom reading. The author informs us that he is content with either judgment—any attention being better than none at all.

We commend this *smörgåsbord* to you and we congratulate Cowley Publications on their whimsical willingness to publish a book that falls, more resolutely than most, between two stools. Given the irony of a God who saves the world by foolishness and weakness, and the hilarity by which he gives us corn, wine, and oil—not to mention his wonderfully two-faced creatures such as butter, salt, tobacco, and pork fat—this is no world in which to land on one side of a paradox. Nibble away, then. You have nothing to lose but your sad, straight face and your narrow waistline.

Pietro and Madeleine, Shelter Island, New York, 2004

one

Fast Shuffle

"I *hate* Lent!" Madeleine fumed. "Who ever dreamed up the dumb idea of having people make themselves miserable for forty days? I can't stand one more minute of it."

Pietro had to deal with the same complaint every year. He decided to try firmness this time. "Let me point out that the amount of Lent on which that childish outburst was based should be an embarrassment to you. This is only Ash Wednesday and you are not even halfway through the altogether delicious tomato soup I made you for supper."

"*You* should be embarrassed! This soup is half heavy cream, at least. You call that fasting? I call it hypocrisy—and high in calories besides. Now if *I* were going to fast . . ."

He cut her off. "That is perhaps the shabbiest argument in the world. It's the old, village-atheist cheap shot: 'I wouldn't be caught dead doing what you're doing; but if I did it, I'd do it all the way.' People who disapprove of an entire discipline have no business offering to improve other people's exercise of it. Furthermore, you misunderstand the point of the Lenten fast."

"It's the Lenten fast that's a misunderstanding. Supposedly, we're saved on the basis of grace and forgiveness, not merit. What's the good of encouraging ourselves to think we can pile up a whole lot of brownie points by fasting?"

"As I was saying," Pietro continued blandly, "the fast is not a matter of getting merit badges for strenuous exertion. It is, to begin with, a *corporate* observance. Just as the faithful join one another in feasting to celebrate the mighty acts they're saved *by*, so they join in fasting to remind themselves of the more depressing stuff they're saved *from*."

"Who needs to fast for that? They could watch the eleven o'clock news."

"Let me finish. Therefore, just as it is not central to the Easter feast, say, for any particular group of the faithful to sound like the Metropolitan Opera chorus or cook on a par with *Lutece*, so it is unnecessary, in the case of the Lenten fast, for them to end up with distended bellies or sunken cheeks. God has arranged for salvation on the basis of no contests at all: not in singing, not in cooking, not in starving—not even, I might add, in deportment. He simply encourages a bit of togetherness when we commemorate the cancellation of such eternal gong shows."

"It's still ridiculous. We make a rule not to have meat on Ash Wednesday, right? So then, instead of eating up the half-pound of old chopped beef in the fridge, we have lobster bisque in honor of the world's miseries. That's okay, huh?"

"Your arguments strike home with all the precision of a cart full of custard pies pushed over a cliff. To begin with, you are eating plain tomato soup, not lobster bisque. I would be flattered if I believed you actually thought it was lobster; but in fact, I suspect this is only another of your red herrings."

"Humph!"

Pietro pressed his advantage. "Next, as to your question. Yes, it is okay. The fast, from the point of view of the individual, is primarily an act of obedience done for the sake of identification with the corporate observance. Therefore any food may be taken that meets the bare requirements of the fast. It need not be nasty, mean, brutish—or even in short supply. It can, in fact, be as delicious as you please and still constitute a fasting meal."

"But *lobster*?"

"Yes, lobster. Of course, lobster. But why are you so fascinated with this *bête rouge* you keep dragging into the discussion? You challenge me to match the sum total of the world's miseries with a fast, but then you complain that I fall short because I have eaten lobster instead of beetles or something. Why, I could starve myself stone cold to death and still fall short. To use your very own argument, the world's miseries are tractable only to God's grace, not my merits. A lobster, obediently ingested, can remind me of that as well as anything else, eaten or not eaten, on the same principle."

Madeleine looked at him intently. "Anything?"

"Absolutely."

"Desserts?"

"Of course."

"Popcorn with TV?"

Pietro hesitated. "I suppose."

"Chocolates?"

"What happened to the hypocrisy of calories?"

"I was just testing you. Can we have wine with dinner?"

"Yes."

"Martinis before? Drambuie after?"

"Yes. Yes."

"All right then, I'll give the fast another try."

Pietro sighed. "But no lobster, right?"

"Of course not. I hate lobster too. What do you think this is, Lent or something?"

two

Fortune Smiles

Pietro hung up the phone and poked his head into the den where Madeleine was knitting. "Prepare to suspend your habit of disbelief," he said; "that was California on the wire."

She eyed him over the tops of her glasses. "I went to high school with a girl named Indiana. This couldn't be her sister, could it?"

"No. As a matter of fact, it was Dame Fortune. A Mr. Michael Yaconelli, who claims to live in some place called Yreka, California, just called with the good news that the powers that be at *The Wittenberg Door* wish me to become a contributor."

"Yaconelii of Yreka," she mused. "Sounds like Rishigan Fishigan from Sishigan Michigan—if you're old enough to re-member the Vic and Sade show."

"Let us not date ourselves, my Dear. *The Wittenberg Door* is one of the few truly open-minded journals on the contemporary theological scene. It actually dares to deal with religion in some-thing other than pulpit tones and wedding-text typefaces."

"It's the *Mad Comics* of evangelicalism, that's what it is. And it's also having a mid-life crisis. Fresh-mouthing the establishment is the hardest act in the world to keep from going stale."

Pietro chose an important chair and sat down. "Be that as it may, I am delighted at the offer."

"I wonder how they thought of you. Hmm . . . I've got it! They were on their way down to the bottom of the barrel and you were rising to the level of your incompetence; the two of you just bumped into each other in mid-drift."

"I prefer," Pietro huffed, "to think of it as a providential meeting of stout, if ribald defenders of the faith on the green uplands of religious journalism."

"Yet another bum rap for Providence."

"Come now, you do admit that the magazine is entertaining, don't you?"

"Yes. It's sort of like getting to spend six nights a year listening to shaggy dog stories. You laugh a lot, but in the morning you wonder what was so funny."

Pietro decided to take another tack. "I shall not even ask your opinion of the magazine's philosophical soundness. When these moods are upon you, nothing is sacred—not even the noble vocation of making hamburger out of sacred cows. I suppose I shall simply have to do without your help in composing my first column."

"Nonsense! I was just warming you up in the bullpen. What's the column supposed to be about?"

"Well, it seems that the editors have anticipated your diagnosis of mid-life creaks in the hinges of the *Door*, so they've agreed that a perceptive piece on the uses and abuses of religious satire might be just the grease they need."

Madeleine folded up her knitting. "Okay, satire it is, then. But remember, the topic can be kiboshed just as easily by ponderousness as by flippancy."

"You leave me only a thin line to tread."

"So? The *Door* has been doing a high-wire act for years."

"Fair enough," Pietro said, cocking an enumerative thumb. "Point number one, I think, will be that satire, like humor in general, works by inducing in its audience a sudden realization of incongruity."

"That's about as light as a truckload of uranium."

"Nevertheless, that means that the most likely targets for both satire and humor will always be things like love, sex, death, politics, and religion. The very gravity and inevitability of such subjects make human beings think that anything they choose to do or say about them will automatically be covered by the veil of their vast importance."

"And?"

"And, since people have an almost inexhaustible talent for doing, in the name of these subjects, things that are tacky, nonsensical, avaricious, or worse, that means that it's fair game for anyone to peek behind the veil and point out the wackiness, wickedness, or whatever."

"But," Madeleine broke in, "shouldn't . . ."

Pietro added a threatening index finger to his still cocked thumb and aimed it at her. "Point number two, if I may proceed, is that the charge of excessiveness usually leveled against satirists is almost always off the mark. Take cheap, funeral parlor poetry, for instance. Take, in fact, the all-time winner in the Uncle-Harry-isn't-really-dead department: the poem whose each and every stanza ends with, 'He's gone upstairs and closed the door.' If people cannot perceive the banal incongruity of that bit of doggerel—if they cannot hear, in their mind's ear, the muffled sound of a commode flushing at the top of the staircase—then they deserve to have it forced upon them by the use of more jarring incongruities still: by an expository apostrophe, for example, that addresses the poem's hero with the words 'C'mon, Harry; aren't you done *yet?*"

"But shouldn't there be some limits to satirical excess?" Madeleine asked. "I mean, how crude can you get?"

"I'm afraid you've got apples and oranges mixed up in that question," Pietro answered. "Let me sort them out before you make marmelsauce of them. As far as excess in satire is concerned, there can be no limits to it at all. Since profound incongruities are already present, unnoticed, in all the solemn follies of the race, the satirist must be as outrageous as possible: otherwise the troops will simply continue to think that chocolate crucifixes, say, or six-foot, inflatable Bibles, are just what the Spirit ordered. But crudity in satire is another matter. In all likelihood there will always be some; but care should be taken to keep it within the limits imposed by the generally accepted but not, alas, clearly defined canons of good taste. On this count, therefore, the satirist must pick his way through a minefield of differing sensibilities. One man's green weenie is another man's . . ."

"Okay, okay. You really think all this pontificating is going to help the *Door*?"

"One can only hope," Pietro replied. "It is my fondest wish that on the score of excess, the *Door* will make a mid-life resolve to become more excessive still—to pile, as it were, extravagance upon outrage upon incongruity—and to heed none of those doctrinaire grouches who clutter up its letters-to-the-editor pages. The Reverend Mr. Yaconelli, young man that he is, can hardly have committed so many sins as to deserve the fractious literary parish he finds himself saddled with."

"Well, maybe," Madeleine conceded. "But what's your wish on the score of crudity?"

"Ah, that. Actually, I find the *Door* to be in downright poor taste refreshingly seldom, considering what the temptations must be. Religion brings out the worst in people, especially magazine readers. Think of all that name-calling, anathema-hurling, and subscription-canceling. Why, it'd be enough to drive even Miss Manners to indelicacy. You'd think their mothers never taught them how to enjoy their toys without beating other kids over the head with them."

"Religion is a *toy?*"

"Listen. If the Wisdom of God can actually call itself foolishness, who's to say the *Door* can't play around a little? Besides, it *is* a middle-aged magazine."

three

Hands On

Madeleine's visitor watched as Pietro added some more flour to the bowl, worked the dough around hard and fast with a spatula and flipped it out onto a board. "You do that so energetically, Peter," she said. "It would wear me out. I always make my bread in the food processor."

He shrugged a smile in Sarah's direction. There was no use arguing with people who put the definite article in front of things only the elect possessed. It was the sign of a mind that had closed itself to all but the most with-it way of getting a job done. People who talked about "*the* ride-on mower," "*the* Caddie," "*the* maid," or *the* food processor" were out of his league. He had *a* mower, *a* Chevy, *no* maid, and *a* blender. How would they describe his breadmaking? By *the* hand?

The usage was pretentious. It implied that everybody had the gadget in question and that if you didn't, you were obviously nobody. There was a place for *the*, of course. You did tell people to bake their bread in *the* oven; but only because that piece of equipment was democratically distributed. But you didn't, un-

11

less you were putting them down, tell ordinary mortgagees and renters to put their scraps into *the* garbage compactor.

Still his objection to trendy kitchen gizmos ran deeper than the merely grammatical. They struck him as profoundly unnecessary. He kept that opinion, however, strictly under his hat. There was no faster way to get yourself drummed out of the food writers' fraternity than to express public doubt about the processor's sovereignty. Indeed, there were probably spies everywhere: just in case they might be bugging him, he decided not to mention its name, even in his own mind. Henceforth, it would be the "F. P."

But in the secrecy afforded by that code, he allowed himself to utter the ultimate treason: the F. P., despite certain undeniable advantages, was N. G. He shuddered. It was the emperor's new clothes all over again, but he was no little boy. He knew what the authorities could do. First, the warnings: a hole mysteriously punched in a strainer here, the seasoning scoured off an iron frying pan there. Then, the surreptitious break-ins, with his recipes scattered and his pencils broken. Finally, the really rough stuff: no more expense account lunches with food editors; and contracts, if any, would be put out *on* him, not mailed *to* him.

Nevertheless, he would not recant. The F. P., at least as he had seen it used, was an instance of gadgetry triumphing over sense. He had watched an otherwise reasonable lady recently as she chopped up an onion. In Pietro's book, that was something you did with a sharp blade on a board. And it took less than forty seconds start to finish, including cleanup. Not so with the lady in question.

Announcing proudly that her F. P. had taken all the work out of chopping onions, she addressed herself to peeling it with the aid of a paring knife. *Aid*, however, was too strong a word. A wooden spoon would have been as much help as the quintessentially dull tool she had in hand. It slipped and slid on the outer paper of the onion without once entering the vegetable itself. Pietro marked down score minus one for the F. P.: its very sharpness absolved people from keeping an edge on anything else in the kitchen. She had to stab the onion to make a dent in it and, even at that, the ends were removed more by prying them off than by cutting.

In just under a minute, though, she had managed to hurt the onion badly enough to reduce it to pieces the F. P. would accept. Then followed the obligatory walk to the other side of the kitchen where she found, predictably, that the shredder plate, rather than the chopping blade, was in the machine. So it was down with the onion, off with the lid and out with the plate— and then back in, back on and back up—till all systems were finally go (score minus two). "Wait till you see how fast this is," she gurgled. "In fact, if you're not careful, it makes mush." (Score minus three.)

It was indeed fast. She was two minutes, one second from starting time when she hit the switch, and at two minutes, three the job was done. Except for the necessity of removing the blade before proceeding (minus four), the hunt for a spatula to get the pieces out of the container (minus five), and the labor of having to wash it up because she had cheese still to grate (minus six).

Pietro thought about the F. P. and bread. He was still kneading his handmade dough, but he had gotten past the point of having to use any more flour on the board. Sarah was no doubt itching to tell him her machine would have the job done by now, but he didn't care. He liked working by feel. The world was full enough of machines that turned him into a minute-minder. He didn't need one between him and his bread.

No doubt the F. P. made a decent product; but besides depriving him of one of the oldest activities of the race, it mired him in the newest of economic problems. Today, for example, he was making four loaves. With the F. P., that would be two energy-intensive trips through the entire mixing and kneading process. The lighting company might be happy to sell him the electricity, but why should he make OPEC rich, when he could do the whole job once—and with no other power than the solar energy he stored up at dinner?

It was, he supposed, just that quality of disproportion that bothered him most. To have to engage great turbines to chop an onion, open a can, or thaw a hot dog was to enter a world whose folly only Rube Goldberg saw clearly: the Candle (J) is extinguished because Latin Husband (A) becomes hot under Celluloid Collar (B) when he sees Wife (C) kissing Lover (D); Collar ignites, setting fire to Tail of Persian Cat (E) who runs off, pulling String (F)—and so on, into the sleep of reason.

There were, to be sure, machines proportionate to their tasks. Pietro had worked with his share of commercial grinders, slicers, mixers, and peelers. And he would dearly love to have a hotel-sized F. P. or a big convection oven at his disposal. But as these things were scaled down for home use, they were not only questionably efficient; worse yet, they scaled up the home itself to the proportions of a factory with not enough to do.

It simply did not take machinery like that to make bread for four people. If the boy-wonder engineers who designed these gadgets wanted to do something useful, let them come up with a decent household gas stove. Pietro could slice, chop, shred and knead as fast as anyone. But he had never been able to produce uniform heat over the bottom of an eleven-inch skillet, at least not with any domestic range he'd ever had. So let them work on that—with no flights of fancy into irrelevancies with instrumentation like a DC-10's. And while they're at it, let them work in a standard-equipment convection oven, twenty-four inches by eighteen, with a bottom you can do pizzas on. F. P. indeed! What good is all the shredded mozzarella in the world if you can't turn out a proper crust?

Pietro finished the kneading, plopped the dough into a bowl, and set it to rise. It was just a matter of time—the mercifully unintensive time of creatures like yeast and flour and fire—before there would be crusty loaves. He and Madeleine, after Sarah had zipped back to her sped-up society, would sit down to a leisurely feast of all eight heels, with a good quarter-pound of honest butter and a bottle of red wine that nobody had rushed.

What would he do with the middles of the loaves? Ah! They were important enough for the definite article. He would wrap them in the plastic and store them in the freezer until they were needed for the roast pork sandwich. And when it was time to reheat them, he would not do it in a microwave, but in the regular oven, in the plain brown paper bag. When it came to the homemade bread, even Pietro was not above being the snob.

four

Creativity

"The subject is a shambles," Pietro said, talking aloud to himself. "The next time anyone mentions the word 'creativity,' I shall insist that the mess be straightened up forthwith. Loose talk like that . . ."

Madeleine interrupted him as he wandered into the kitchen. "You know I can't hear you when the dishwasher's running," she complained. "Especially if you mumble. The only words I actually got were 'creativity' and 'loose talk.'"

Pietro looked stunned. "It's an act of Providence!" he declared, dramatically switching off the dishwasher. "Not ten seconds ago, I took a vow to give a stern lecture on creativity to the next person who so much as mentioned the subject, and here you stand . . ."

"Oh, wow!" she said cynically. "I feel like one of those characters in a Greek tragedy. I make an innocent mistake like asking somebody what he just said, and this horrible, predetermined fate comes crashing down on me."

Pietro fixed her with a stern, faraway look. "We are all of

us, my dear, mere threads upon a loom that weaves a tissue vaster than our designs. A vow is a vow, a fateful knot in the tapestry of time."

"Will you stop with the echo-chamber philosophy and wah-wah prose," Madeleine said exasperatedly. "Talk about loose talk! You sound like an ad from an occult gem catalogue."

"I did rather catch the tone, didn't I?" Pietro said, pleased with himself.

"Will you also stop with this game-playing inside your own head," she exclaimed. "If you want to talk to me about creativity, I'll give you five minutes. Otherwise, I go back to work and you go on getting lost in the back alleys of your mind."

"Good," Pietro said, husbanding his powers of distinction. "Creativity. Hmmm. Let me be as methodical as possible."

"Permission granted," she said. "You have also just used up ten seconds."

"Spur me on, then, and I shall be speedy as well. Point one: strictly speaking, to create means to bring into being out of nothing. Therefore only God creates, and only God can correctly be called creative."

Madeleine applied the spur promptly: "What then are we to call the people we used to call creative?"

"We are to call them *makers* rather than creators."

"Isn't that a comedown?"

"Not at all," Pietro said. "The Greek for 'to make' is *poiein*, from which we get 'poet.' If anything, therefore, it is a comeup. Whether we make mudpies or machines, noodles or novels, we are all poets."

"What about when we make babies?"

"Ah," Pietro said, taking exception. "Strictly speaking, *we* don't make babies; our bodies, guided by our DNA—with the entire process, of course, guided ultimately by God—are the only agents capable of that kind of manufacture. That is why the act is properly called *pro*creation: when we conceive a child we are neither creators nor poets, we are minor agents acting on behalf of principals beyond our ken."

Madeleine dug in the spur again. "Tantivvy! Hoicks!" she cried. "No slowing down like that. What about creativity not-strictly-speaking? What about originality? What, in short, about the categories of artistic criticism?"

Pietro sized up the hedge and took it at a bound. "Originality is a goal no artist ought ever to set herself. Let critics decide after she is dead whether or not her work was unique or new; while she lives, let her seek only to be *good* at what she does. Conscious striving after originality produces nothing but predictably weird hairdos."

"C'mon boy," Madeleine said, applying the whip. "Giddyap! Get that hair out of your eyes!"

Pietro leapt into the next subject. "Creativity not-strictly-speaking," he declaimed. A legitimate category. We are made in the image of the Creator, and specifically in the image of the creating Word, the Second Person of the Trinity. Therefore, when we use words to shape our world—as we do not only when we make books and ballads but also when we make duck soup and gasoline, mansard roofs and French doors—we come marvelously close to making something out of nothing. This is clearest in music and literature: a sonata comes, seemingly, 'out of the nowhere into the here'; a novel is a complete world handed to the reader practically *ex nihilo*. But a harpsichord or a double-hung window, a dish of *tripe Nicoise* or a computer spreadsheet program are no less manifestations of the power by which our words have effect beyond our powers."

"Good boy," Madeleine murmured, sparing the stick and proffering the carrot. "That was a lot of ground to cover in a short time. Head for the barn and I'll give you sugar lumps."

"But the root of all creativity," Pietro said proceeding headlong, "whether of the divine, strictly *ex nihilo* variety or of the human, less-strict, out-of-thin-air sort, is one thing and one thing only: delight. The great world exists because it is the apple of God's eye—because he says 'Good!' (or, more accurately, '*Tov meod!*') to it after every day and every moment of its triumphant leap out of nothing into being at his voice. And the lesser worlds we make by words—our *poiêmata*, our *poems*, whether of science, art, or craft—all likewise exist because somewhere a poet could be found to speak them into the dance of her delight . . ."

"Whoa, boy!" Madeleine said breathlessly. "You made it! Now tell me honestly, wasn't that a whole lot better than fuming to yourself about the subject?"

Pietro looked puzzled. "Yes, I guess it was," he said. "It must be Providence again, working things out so nicely."

"Providence, my eye," Madeleine shot back. "I heard every word you mumbled back there. I mentioned 'creativity' just to give you a break with your silly vow."

"That could still be providence," Pietro said creatively. "I never said *whose*."

five

No Job at All

Pietro heard her the minute he switched off the ignition. Through two closed doors, yet. Madeleine was in what he had come to recognize as intermediate dudgeon.

He gathered up the grocery bags and struggled out of the car into the breezeway. Since she reserved her full fury for tirades at the children, he concluded from this half-throttle performance that it was a friend's ear, not theirs, she was bending on the subject of teenage derelictions. Sarah's, no doubt. It was always Sarah, the perpetual visitor. He would have to face not one but two irate mothers.

He angled himself through the kitchen door and just made it to the counter as eight chickens dropped through the bottom of the bag. "A very good day to you both," he said brightly. "I come in peace with healing in my wings—or at least with wings of healing falling all over the counter. Give me two hours to cut up these birds, and we'll have chicken soup. Balm for hoarse maternal throats." Direct response to wrathful indignation was not his way. Whipping out a cutting board and a Chinese cleaver, he smiled approvingly. "Forty-nine cents a pound. I couldn't resist."

"Do you have to make a mess in here now?" Madeleine objected. "I was just beginning to calm down after cleaning up the filth those house apes of yours left. They shouldn't be allowed in a bathroom. Even a privy would be too good for them."

Pietro walked over and kissed both women—in the approved matrimonial order: Sarah last. "Never fear, Mr. Neat is here. Can I fetch either of you a drop of the milk of human kindness in the form of jug Chablis? That way, we can all sip while I dismantle these featherless fowls." It was a safe offer. Sarah had yet to refuse her first glass of wine.

"I'd love some," she said. "And so would Madeleine. She's had a hard afternoon." As he poured the wine, Sarah eyed the chickens on the counter. "Say, what *are* you going to do with all those?"

Pietro placed the first two birds on the board, took the sharpening steel off its hook, and touched up the cleaver with a few light strokes. "I am going to reap the fruits of this largesse by doing my own butchering. Watch and be amazed. By the time these have been cut up and boned out, my original twelve-and-a-half dollar investment will have a market value of thirty dollars at least."

"I know, I know," she sighed. "But it's such a job. I'd never have the patience for it."

He was tempted to say more, but the air was already thick enough with correction. He simply thought his rejoinders to himself as he chopped off the wings of bird number one.

Listen, Honey Child, he mused (his interior dialogues were always more aggressive than his conversations). The first reason you think it's such a project is that you never stopped whimpering long enough to learn how to sharpen a knife. Come around some time with an open mind, a stone, and a steel, and

I'll show you how to save enough money to cover your wine budget for the rest of your life.

He turned the chicken end for end, made a cut on each side of the body, popped out the hip joints with a decisive downward bend of the legs, and sliced them off smartly. He repeated the wing and leg operation on birds two through eight as he thought further.

And the next reason why you think it's a big deal, Ducks, is that you are a Pisces with Gemini ascending who can't stick to one operation at a time. On second thought, don't come around. Eight chickens might just take you till the Rapture.

He looked at Madeleine before boning out the breasts. She seemed calmer, thanks to the Brothers Gallo, so he decided to risk a small involvement on her part. "Do you think, Love, that you might be kind enough to bag up these parts while I continue? Many hands, and all that." Hearing no objection, he passed her the plastic wrap.

"Did I say yes? Since when do we allow the argument from silence around here?"

"It's not from silence, it's from Eliot," he retorted. "I am 'One of the low on whom assurance sits / Like a silk hat on a Bradford millionaire.' I make a welcome of indifference."

She smiled at last. "Watch out, or I'll wrap you. Hand me the parts."

Pietro bowed and returned to his cutting. He pulled the skin from the breast and boned out the fillets of one bird after another.

But third and finally, he told his mental Sarah as he worked, your biggest mistake is your failure to distinguish a job from a habit. You think I don't know what Madeleine was bewailing when I came in. But you are wrong. She was in a fit over the fact that her children (you see, I can shift ownership of them as well as she) make the very same mistake apropos the bathroom as you do anent the kitchen.

There are tasks in life, he continued inwardly, which when considered as jobs are nothing but burdens. If, however, you can manage to relegate their performance to habit, they practically accomplish themselves.

Take these children, for example, whose untidiness has led you to disrupt the tranquility of my kitchen in my absence. To them, the bathroom is an Augean stable that they can bring themselves to cleanse only upon threat of bodily harm or durance vile. Thus crippled in their thinking, they fail to see that if they would acquire three simple habits—wiping out the sink, hanging up the towel, and removing the hair from the tub strainer—their mother would never even suspect they used the bathroom at all.

So, too, Dear Benighted Sarah, with yourself. This boning out of chickens, which to you seems nothing less than all the labors of Hercules combined, is to me no more than a habit. Dismembering birds is something I do when I walk in the house with them—just as my taking off of galoshes is occasioned by my coming in from the rain. I do not think in either case about the process or about the time required. I simply do it.

And there at last is the reason why, even though you admire the largesse of my kitchen and nosh your way through whole afternoons of my soup, chicken salad, and rice pudding, you will never duplicate them for yourself. These things are not work. They hardly even deserve the name of dishes. They are culinary standing orders, nothing more.

Chicken soup is a reflex response to the presence of carcasses most people throw away. And the onion, celery tops, and parsley stems you make it with come from trimmings you routinely store in a bag in the freezer. Chicken salad is what happens automatically when you pick over the soup bones before you throw them to the dogs. And rice pudding occurs, not because you decided to get out a recipe, but because you customarily boil leftover rice with milk, sugar, vanilla, and a little grated lemon rind—and keep adding milk every time you walk past it, until it's wet enough.

But without such habits as those, Dear Girl, you will never make it as one who cooks with ease and *eclat*. It delights me to think that this very evening, while you and your household suffer through some tuna-noodle job of work, we shall be feasting here on an offhand bonus from this saving routine: lightly sautéed chicken breasts finished with shallots, Madeira, cream, and a couple of cubes of homemade *glace de viande*. What's that? Meat glaze, Kiddo, There's a *real* habit: it takes the better part of two days, and it uses up a stack of pots. But it's a blessing you'll never know.

Madeleine interrupted his reverie. "Sarah invited us over for a late supper tonight. Are we free to go? She says Murray has a couple of bottles of Claret he just came across. What did you say it was, Sarah?"

"*Chateau Margaux* 1961. I think. I don't know what to have with it, but I'll think of something. Can you come, Peter?"

Pietro suddenly applied the brakes to his afternoon's train of thought. "Why thank you, Sarah. We'd love to."

Convictions be damned, he reflected to himself. After all, '61 Margaux *was* '61 Margaux.

s i x

Simple Dictation

"The trouble with you," Madeleine snapped . . .

Pietro interrupted. "Dr. Grimtruth, the noted marriage counselor, says that the word *you* should be outlawed in domestic disputes."

"Dr. Grimtruth doesn't live with y—"

"Tch, tch," Pietro said. "That was almost another one. The good doctor says the only way to cure the addiction is to swear off the word, cold turkey—as I am doing, please note—and begin every complaint with the first person singular."

"Oh, all right," she snapped. "*I* think the trouble with you is—"

"Still a no-no," he said. "That's just a transparent attempt to have it both ways. Try again."

"I don't have to," she said triumphantly. That's exactly what I was going to say."

"That I'm trying to have it both ways?"

"Precisely."

"How?"

"By complaining that nobody ever responds to food columns, and then not answering letters when people do write to y—"

"I wasn't complaining," Pietro broke in. "I was propounding my theory that writing for publication is like putting notes in bottles and throwing them in the ocean."

"That's not a theory, it's a one-liner."

"But it's the truth."

"Not when letters come back, it isn't. Look. I'll even take dictation and type out the replies"—Madeleine finally gave up avoiding the word—"if only you will stay put and attend to business. Sit! I'm about to begin."

Pietro considered his options and sat. "How many letters are there?"

"As a matter of fact, only one. It's about . . ."

"One? You said *letters.*"

"I meant correspondence. It's about your column on meat glaze."

"Ah! *Glace de viande,*" Pietro mused. "The soul of meat. The sovereign cure for insipid pan gravies, dull chops, and pallid fish. I think I may have just enough scraps around to . . ."

"Hold!" Madeleine commanded. "Give me five minutes and you can go dig for old bones to your heart's content."

"Arf," Pietro replied meekly.

"That's better," she said, holding up a fat letter; "This one is from Michelle Predatore in Copiague, Long Island. She wants to know how to make it. I just hope it's meat glaze she has in mind."

Pietro stared at the folded sheets in her hand. "Hey! That's got to be four pages, at least. It took her all that to ask *how?*"

"No. In the first sentence—which runs on to the bottom of page three—she says she's dying to meet you."

"I don't get to answer that part? Even if the poor girl is dying?"

"Don't let it worry you. Everybody has to go sometime. Just give her the recipe."

Pietro sighed. "How about I dictate only an outline? It can get turned into English on the typewriter, okay?"

"By whom?"

"By y—" Pietro almost slipped. "By the typist, of course. Remind me to thank this typist person some day. But back to Michelle. First, tell her to freeze all the bones and meat scraps she can get her hands on: beef, pork, veal, or chicken—cooked or raw, fat, skin, and all—anything but lamb or smoked stuff. Then, when she has fifteen or twenty pounds, tell her to brown them in a baking pan in a 400-degree oven for maybe two hours. The last half-hour or so, she should add some cut-up onion, carrot and celery—two really big ones of each—and let them brown, too. But not *blacken*. Underscore that, okay?"

"Sure. But two really big *whats* of celery? Whole bunches or single stalks?"

"Singles; in the food-writing business, we call them 'ribs.' Anyway, when it's all nice and brown, she empties the contents of the pan into a big pot—say, twenty or thirty quarts. Then she puts some cold water in the baking pan and heats it on top of the stove, scraping the pan to dissolve all the browning. Next, she pours the water into the pot with the meat and bones, and she puts in enough additional cold water to cover everything by about two inches. Finally, she adds a little thyme, savory, marjoram, and bay leaf, brings it all to a boil, and then turns the heat to very low, covers it, and lets it simmer for five, maybe six hours."

"You want salt in there?"

"Oh, boy. Lucky we caught that. Tell her, in caps and underscored: <u>NO SALT</u>. Now then. When she's done, she strains off the liquid and refrigerates it overnight till the fat hardens."

"The fat on what? The broth or the strainings? I think you have to be clear with Michelle."

"*That* clear? Well, tell her what she's after is the broth—the leavings are dog food. Anyway, in the morning, she removes the fat completely, brings the broth back to a fast boil, and boils it down, uncovered, till it's a viscous, burnished-brown liquid."

"I don't know about Michelle and 'viscous.' Say it another way."

Well, tell her she's got to reduce it all the way down from about a gallon to about a pint. Then she pours it into an ice cube tray *without dividers or partitions*—got that emphasis?—and she puts it in the *refrigerator*, not the freezer, for another overnight stay. When it's *good and cold*, she takes it *out of the tray* by lifting up *one end* with a *fork* and *pulling it out* like a *rubber beach-sandal sole*."

"What if it breaks?"

"Believe me, it won't. Then she cuts it with a *knife* . . ." Pietro hesitated. "Listen. Aren't we being just a little *too* clear with Michelle? I mean, it's beginning to sound *insulting*."

"I want clarity about that, too."

"Oh, well. She cuts it into *cubes* with a *knife*, plops them into a *baggie*, ties it with a *twisty*, and stores them in the *left hand end* of the *top shelf* of her *freezer door*. All those italics will even tell her what they'll be good for."

"They will?"

"Sure. It will make her cooking *emphatic*. What else? May I go?"

"You *could* thank the typist."

"Oh, all right," Pietro said, his mind already out in the kitchen. "Thank you."

"Aha!" Madeleine crowed. "You finally said it! For that last word, I thank *you*."

seven

Unlocking the Mystery of Menus

"What I want to know," Madeleine said as she fastened her seat belt, "is how you always manage to pick the best dish on the menu. It's infuriating, you know. People ask you for advice, but you never say a word. You just sit there till everybody else has ordered and then quietly one-up them. It's amazing anyone still takes us out to dinner."

Pietro backed the car out of the restaurant parking lot and headed home. Amazing or not, it was lucky someone had taken him this time. He'd gotten a look at the bill: $120 for four. Their host had admittedly been valiant at running up the bar tab, but even so, the food had come to about $65. It was all good, though. The chef knew what he was doing—and Pietro had enough insight into the trade to know that, in spite of the prices, he wasn't getting rich at it. Still, Madeleine apparently expected an answer.

"Nonsense," he chided. "Nobody could have stopped you and Sally from ordering *tournedos Perigordine*. I admit that $15 for a fillet mignon with itty-bits of truffle is not my idea of how to spend money in a restaurant; but if Henry wasn't quibbling over figures, why should I? Besides, I did think the sauce was nice work: no commercial bases and just the right touch of Madeira. And Henry's liver—at least the piece he had on his plate—was perfect. How can you complain?"

"I can complain because I tasted what you had. It was heavenly. And it was practically the cheapest thing on the menu. What's the name again?"

"*Brandade de morue.* You soak a piece of dried salt cod in several changes of cold water for twelve hours. Then you boil it for a while, pick the flesh off the bones, pound the daylights out of it till it's nothing but threads, put it over the fire and beat in lots of olive oil, heavy cream and garlic. You don't seriously think though, that if I had said all that before they ordered, they would have sprung for it, do you? I can just hear Sally now: 'Oh, codfish? Yecch!' If she wants to worship at the shrine of high-priced goodies, who am I to interfere with her religion? Besides, she was right in a way: it was an odd item to find as an entree on a dinner menu. As an appetizer, maybe; but basically it's a luncheon dish. Peasant food."

"Is that what you do," Madeleine pressed, "order peasant food? What if they don't offer any, though? You still end up with the best-tasting meal. Tell me how you really do it."

Pietro had no ready answer for that. He worked mostly by instinct when it came to food. At home, he would estimate quantities for a party dinner not by formula but by going into a kind of mystic trance in front of the rice pot or the potato bin. When his sixth sense said "too much," or "not enough" he reacted accordingly. A lot of that, he supposed, depended on experience; but it remained a heavily psychic exercise.

Experience no doubt entered into his restaurant ordering, too; but there was less of an air of mystery about his eventual choices. For one thing, he knew he regularly used Peter Sichel's price rule not only for wine but for food as well. Sichel said to start at the bottom and order the second from the cheapest wine in the category you wanted. The idea was that the proprietor kept the cheapest one on hand just to satisfy the budget-conscious, but he offered the next one up because he liked it himself and invested heavily in it.

Applied to food, that principle led you to skip over the rock-bottom *Poulet a la Quelquechose* at $6.50: it might be great chicken in a terrific sauce, but if the chef could do that for the penny-wise, he might well have something spectacular up his sleeve for those who were not automatically pound-foolish. You moved up to the $8.25 plateau, therefore, and looked around.

What precisely did you look for? Well, for one thing, you ruled out anything that was not made on the premises. It was the rare Breast of Chicken Kiev nowadays that didn't come from a freezer in Arkansas. But second, even when you had spotted the items that were the chef's own work, you tried to zero in on the ones into which he had put a little more effort than shaking the fry basket or fingering a steak on the grill. You looked, in short, for what the British call "made" dishes.

When Pietro chose an appetizer, for example, the principle worked perfectly. He ruled out the cheapest ones—the broiled grapefruit that went down like hot battery acid, and the canned fish and jarred herring he could buy at the supermarket. Moving up the price scale, however, he likewise skipped the snails, which were almost certainly not prepared from scratch in the kitchen, and the marinated mushrooms and artichoke hearts, which could have been picked up down the street at the Italian pork store. That left the chef's own concoctions: things like *Brandade de Morue* and, of course, the ever-present bellwether of the kitchen's capabilities, the *pâté*.

In fact, Pietro was of the opinion that a wise diner should, if he could get away with it, order his entree only after he had eaten the appetizer. If the *pâté* turned out to be nothing more than chopped liver with a shot of cognac, he would be forewarned to opt for fried soft-shelled crabs as a main course—or, if they were frozen instead of live, for a piece of grilled striper, or anything for that matter, that hadn't seen too many sunrises from a truck. But if the *pâté* was . . . well, if it was indeed *pâté*, then anything else the chef put both hands to would probably be worth putting money on.

So it wasn't simply peasant food he chose. If he did that often, it was because things like *cassoulet*, *choucroute garni*, and *tripe Nicoise* promised him more of the cook's mind and heart than *tournedos* ever could. And, to take up Madeleine's original charge, if he didn't usually help people with advice about their food orders, he regularly tipped them on wines. Why, this very evening he had saved his host from financial ruin. Henry had been about to take the plunge for a small year of a big-name Claret with a price that practically ran off the card; the 1969 *St. Estephe* that Pietro had eventually suggested provided them with two bottles for less than the price of one.

Madeleine could think what she liked. It wasn't that he tried to one-up people. It was that somehow they were more open to advice about wine than about food. Probably because since childhood they'd had more than their fill of lectures on the subject. They didn't need free-loading guests who reminded them of Daddy. He would continue his practice of ordering last, even if she did find it infuriating. Besides, who made it a rule he shouldn't try to be one-up?

It wasn't every night in the week that Henry could buy dinner for someone who did it without putting him down.

eight

Mystery Train

"Dreadful phrase!" Pietro muttered, pouring a half-pint of heavy cream into a skillet.

"What phrase?" Madeleine asked. "Cholesterol poisoning? Caloric overkill?"

"No. 'Substance abuse.' Too vague. Too sweeping. Too nasty-nice. People want to talk about cigarette smoking, coke-sniffing, and beer-guzzling, but they can't resist the temptation to gussy up their pronouncements with quasi-scientific generalities."

"Am I supposed to get on this train of thought, or should I just let it rattle through the tunnel of your mind?"

Pietro caught himself and turned off the heat under the pan. "Oh. Sorry. Welcome aboard."

"Do I dare ask where we're going?"

"No, it's a surprise. Let me continue. *Abuse*, of course, is a pejorative I can live with. It bears implicit witness to the truth that there is, if we but had the intelligence and the moderation to seek it out, some legitimate use for the things being abused. But *substance*? That gives the impression that everything under the sun, by virtue of its mere materiality, is a hazard. It's positively Manichaean."

"Oh, come on now." Madeleine said. "They're just using the word as a catch-basket so they don't have to run through the whole list of specific addictions every time they address the subject."

"Possibly. But generalities that glitter are rarely gold. In this particular case, *substance* is pure lead. America has a dangerous tendency to think that people's problems can be solved by swearing off things. It deludes itself into believing that if everyone would go cold turkey on tobacco, wine, whiskey, eggs, salt, meat, butter, cream, sugar—and, for all I know, parsley roots and turnip tops—the millennium would arrive."

Madeleine interrupted him. "I don't know about the millennium, but cutting the heavy cream out of your sauces might keep some fat from arriving on my hips."

"God invented cream. Furthermore, having made us in his image, he means us to share his delight in its excellence. Moderation, not abstinence, is the way God intends for us to keep clear of unwanted side effects."

"'That's all very well," Madeleine snapped, "but it's got precious little to do with the problem that the phrase *substance abuse* was coined to deal with. Moderation is for people without problems; we're talking about people who are hooked. Stop trying to worm your way off the subject. What about addiction?"

Pietro took a moment to gather his forces. "All right. Addiction. The first kind is physical, or psychophysical: an individual's system, bodily and/or psychically, becomes so dependent on, say, cigarettes or cocaine that his or her very constitution becomes a conspirator against its own well-being. The second kind is social: the individual's surroundings—friends, media, and so on—conspire to sell him or her on the idea that the gratifications of a particular excess are somehow less threatening than its inevitable consequences. In Marlboro country, for example, the fresh air wafting around the horseback rider distracts the mind from the carcinogens in his lungs. Needless to say, the two addiction-oriented phenomena commonly go hand in hand, with the second leading to the first: peer pressure inveigles teenagers into smoking cigarettes, and habit takes over from there."

"But aren't there some substances—you just mentioned cigarettes—that are inevitably addictive? Isn't smoking a habit that is, at least incipiently, always out of control?"

"I doubt that. Immoderate use is what is addictive. One cigarette a month, even for a lifetime, is probably no danger at all."

"For crying out loud," Madeleine huffed. "You're talking about a kind of smoking that practically no one goes in for. Address the problem!"

"The very thing I am about to do," Pietro said quietly. "My point is simply that demonizing things that can become addictive is not the way to deal with addiction. Nor is it any better to harp on the sinfulness of addicted people. Addiction is a pathology and does not yield to medical or moral lectures. The hooked need help, not harangues. Look at AA. It works, but not by denigrating either wine or winos. What it does is invite drunks to avail themselves of an environment of support—from God, from the group—that is radically non-condemning. And it works best when all the condemning entities—from the family, to the government, to the church—keep their blue noses out of the act."

"Totally?"

"Totally. People who have lost all rational interest in prohibiting themselves unwise excesses find it a cinch to work their way around prohibitions imposed from the outside. As you said of moderation, proscribing substance or behavior patterns works only on people without problems."

"The government shouldn't make marijuana or heroin illegal, then?"

"It can if it wants to—and maybe the proscription would even be a good policy for society at large. But it certainly won't help those already addicted, and it probably won't even do much to slow down the production of new addicts."

"And the church shouldn't declare drunkenness or the cocaine habit sinful?"

"The church, too, can do what it wants. But ditto everything I just said about the government. Just don't let's kid ourselves into thinking that ecclesiastical jawboning is going to be much real help to anybody."

Madeleine stuck to her guns. "But if certain behavior is wrong, doesn't the church have an obligation to tell people so? And aren't even parents under the same obligation to help their children say No to cigarette smoking?"

"They certainly may do so as representatives of the Friend of Sinners," Pietro said as he turned the heat back on under the skillet; "but not, I think, at the price of giving the world the impression that either the church's or the family's principal business is sin-prevention. God in Jesus didn't prevent sinners from sinning, he went around forgiving them right and left. If we want to represent him, we shouldn't misrepresent his methods. We should instead busy ourselves with the twin jobs of forgiveness and healing—with, in short, the Gospel work of raising the dead by laying down our lives for our friends. The world is not a collection of good listeners waiting for the right advice to come down the track; it's a bunch of corpses totally immune to talk. Its resurrection is not in the least facilitated by a surgeon-general's warning that sin should have been avoided in the first place."

"I am risen and reconciled, then, even if all the cream in that sauce makes me fat?"

"Cream doesn't make you fat. Immoderation does. But in the Mystery of Christ, you are absolved even of that."

"What about help and healing, though? Maybe I'm hooked. Maybe you are, too."

"In that case," Pietro said soothingly, we shall get off this Mystery train at the very next stop and form a chapter of creamaholics anonymous. Tomorrow night, no fat in the sauce. But remember, it's only us forgiven sinners who created the problem—not this bubbling, satiny cream."

nine

The Secret Cream Club

Pietro transferred the roasted chicken to a warm platter and put the pan on the stove. He turned the burner up high, poured in some chicken stock and proceeded to boil most of it away, stirring energetically to loosen the browning.

"I always add the flour first" Sally said as she hovered nearby. "Otherwise, it gets all lumpy."

Pietro refilled his dinner guest's vermouth glass while he cast about in his mind for a reply. The words *the flour* betrayed an assumption on her part that sauces could be thickened with nothing else. He decided to disabuse her gently of that notion before informing her that he was about to bind this sauce with heavy cream. One prejudice at a time.

"You're absolutely right," he said, sounding a positive note. "There's no other way. People do, of course, thicken sauces with flour mixed in cold stock or water, but that cuts down the flour's ability to bind the grease. Flour in the fat first is the only way to go . . ."

"But you just put liquid in first."

"So I did. But I also did not finish my sentence. It's the

only way to go . . . provided you intend to use flour for the job."

"Oh, I see," Sally said. "You're making unthickened gravy."

"No," Pietro replied evenly. "This will be thickened and bound to perfection."

"But how," she asked. "Cornstarch?"

"Nope," he said. "Just watch."

He strained the liquid from the pan into a pot, poured in half a pint of heavy cream and set it over high heat.

"A whole container!" she exclaimed. "I've heard about you and heavy cream, but this is unreal. Besides, I thought you weren't supposed to boil cream."

"That, my dear, is an old—or I suppose we should say *new* wives' tale. Old wives have been boiling cream for centuries."

"But doesn't it curdle or something?"

"Negative again, " he answered. "Not only doesn't it curdle, but as it boils down to a proper thickness, it also binds the free fat nicely. The result? A cream sauce that actually tastes like cream instead of diluted wallpaper paste."

"But at that rate, haven't you practically doubled the amount of fat in the sauce?"

"At last I can give you an affirmative. But just think about it for a moment. You are witnessing a kitchen miracle by which grease is bound with more grease. I can't say I understand the chemistry involved, but as you can see, it works like a charm."

"But think of the calories—the strain on the gall bladder!"

"If I were condemned to think about such grim things," Pietro replied, "I would, of course, skim off the fat entirely and serve the unthickened gravy you first suspected me of. However," he said, leaning toward her with a conspiratorial smile, "since none of us here tonight is under so grim a sentence, we shall thumb our noses at the apostles of leanness and live off the fat of the land."

Pietro interrupted himself to taste the sauce. "Ah," he

sighed. "Cream. A creature unjustly maligned. Do you know that there is an evil campaign afoot in this country to deprive us of it altogether? Think of what you get on your dessert in most restaurants—even in most people's houses. Pressurized, fatless foam. And that's if you're lucky. Otherwise you get the crowning insult: non-dairy whipped non-topping.

"But that's not all. Suppose you decide to take up arms against the plot and serve honest whipped cream with your *Apfelkuchen*. When you go to the market what do you find? Nothing but ultrapasteurized cream—which is only slightly easier to whip than tap water."

Pietro put on the most paranoid look he could manage and lowered his voice. "Do you know, Sally, what they *do* to ultra-pasteurized cream? They murder millions of perfectly friendly bacteria—harmless little fellows who otherwise would predispose the cream to cooperate with whisks and beaters. And do you know *why* they do that, Sally? If you think it's for your protection or mine, you're wrong. It's just so the stuff can stay in their profit-seeking dairy cases for weeks instead of days. Oh, perfidy! Oh, shamelessness!"

Sally took a step backwards, looking alarmed.

He tasted the sauce again and waved his wooden spoon menacingly in front of her. "And as if that weren't enough, even if you do manage to get your hands on some plain old pasteurized heavy cream, they poison your mind against it with talk about calories and saturated fats. I tell you, Sally. These are the last days of honest eating. "I wasn't going to mention this till after dinner, but tonight you're going to be invited into the resistance movement. This may look like nothing more than a few people coming to a dinner party, but actually it's a *cell* of the heavy cream underground. The anti-cream forces are all around us. We're not safe, even here.

"Do you know what I found in my refrigerator just the other day?" he said, practically whispering in her ear. "In my very own refrigerator? Standing right next to my grandmother's cut crystal cream pitcher? An aerosol cream can, Sally! They broke and entered in the middle of the night and put it there! It used to be that a person's refrigerator was as safe as a bank. People even hid rolls of bills in the crisper and made jokes about cold cash. But no more, Sally; no more. Nothing's sacred now . . ."

Madeleine came in to the kitchen as Sally abruptly excused herself. Pietro bent over the stove and added another pinch of salt to the sauce.

"I was going to ask you how long till dinner," Madeleine said after Sally was out of the room. "But first I want to know what on earth you've been saying to that poor girl. She looks as if she'd just seen a horror movie."

Pietro strove for a look of innocence. "We were simply talking about cooking, Love. Somehow, she got me onto the subject of heavy cream; but when I started to warm to it, she suddenly went all funny. You know. Nervous. Of course, I may have laid it on just a tad too thick . . ."

"You didn't," Madeleine groaned.

Pietro nodded sheepishly.

"Not the Ernie Kovacs Secret Cream Club act?" she sighed.

"Not all of it," he said. "She left before I could get past the scary part."

ten

Cheeseburger, Cheeseburger

Pietro's cover was blown. Head down, coat collar up, he made it safely through the wait at the not-so-fast food counter, only to be caught by them at the door. He could anticipate Madeleine's crowing now. "That was Sally on the phone with her on-the-spot-reporter's scoop of the week: 'You'll never guess who Murray and I ran into with a bag of burgers in his hand. The chef himself!'"

It was only a matter of time, of course, before his nocturnal noshings would catch up with him; but this was humiliating. Just last night, he had produced a Chinese feast for them: Steamed Eggs with Oysters, Spare Ribs with Black Bean, Beef with Orange Flavor, Chicken with Almonds. Pride before a fall. When Pietro took a header, it wasn't from a basement window.

Still, the experience shouldn't be a total loss. He was halfway through his second cheeseburger when it occurred to him that perhaps there was a philosophical buck somewhere in this gastronomic bankruptcy. Time to drop the dim view of what everybody—himself included—had crowned with success. Try instead to understand.

Why, he wondered, do we eat so much of what we think so little? Hunger as the best sauce? Impulse as the most liberating form of consumption? TV's iron grip upon the mind? All of the above, probably—with maybe an edge given to plain old hunger. He had long felt that the biggest roadblock to the enjoyment of great cooking was the fact that people sat down to it already full.

He hated dinner at eight. Guests arrived at seven, half-stuffed with Spaghetti-O's filched from children's suppers, and then dawdled away the next hour topping themselves up with bacon-wrapped water chestnuts. When they finally got to the table, it was "Just a teeny bit for me, please" and "No rice, thank you, I've got to get back to a size ten." Pietro filed that away under the heading of Dialogue Never Heard at McDonald's.

There had to be more to it. Wiping his mouth after the last carefully reserved central bite of burger, he felt the old urge to go back in for one more. With the desperate honesty of the discovered sinner, he admitted what that meant: you can't order just one more. Fries and another coke are essential to the experience. Maybe that was it. The key was the nature of the experience.

He thought of other pleasures to which he was given. Winebibbing, for one. Someone once divided wines into *sip* and *swallow* types: a single taste of a complex and elegant claret was more than equal to a huge gulp of something merely alcoholic and red. How about the same distinction between foods? *Taste* foods versus *gobble* foods. The second appeases the hunger of the stomach for filler, but the first satisfies the longing of the mind for fascination. Drive-in food is gobble food. The fast feeders fill the hungry with good (?) things, but the mind they send empty away.

But that wouldn't wash. Fast food is not devoid of taste. It was precisely the tickled palate, not the glutted stomach, that was tempting him back to the den of iniquity. Pietro had read somewhere that the largest sexual organ in the body was the brain. How much is too much—or even if more is possible at all—is the work of the mind to decide; the body, even in a state of near-collapse, meekly follows suit. So too with eating. We get fat from the head down. The hamburger has a half-nelson on the mind.

How though? He thought of another of his vices, smoking. Cigarettes were the equivalent of gobble food, the chips and dips of the inhaling public. The need for the weed, once established, was a raw hunger to be appeased by any old smoke at all. Cigars, on the other hand, like a perfect beef bouillon, engaged the critical faculties. They were taste from start to finish, a richness to be sipped and relished at leisure. But pipe smoking? Ah! There was the analogy.

Pipe smoking, contrary to the benign imaginings of bystanders, was neither the simple satisfaction of a physical desire, nor the ruminative enjoyment of an unqualified delight. It was a quest for the elusive but all rewarding taste that comes once in every twenty pipe-fulls—and only in the middle of that one.

What Pietro's mind was doing, therefore, when it commanded his teeth to sink into yet another construct of meat, pickle, cheese, onion, ketchup, sauce, and seedy bun, was flogging his body onward in the quest for taste. Where though, in these unlikely haunts, did taste lie hidden? Certainly not in the parts. Not in the impacted patty, nor in the resolutely middling garnishes taken one by one. Nor was it, in any simple sense, in the whole: these millstones in the stomach were, most of them, only milestones on the mind's road to taste, not arrivals at it.

Where then did it spring from, this fascination for which the mind was willing to kill his reputation to begin with and his body in as long as it took? Pietro sprang from his car. Sally and Murray be damned! He had it! He would stride in proudly for another.

The fatally tempting taste lay, he realized at last, in that final, perfect mouthful he had conjured up by a judicious re-serving of coke, pickle, onion and cheese for a triumphant jux-taposition with the ultimate bite of meat in its ketchup-soaked doily of bread. No matter that it was not in the thirty bites be-fore that—or that it might not be producible in a hundred yet to come. It was possible, and that was enough. "We beat on, boats against the current." Hope was all that mattered.

Maybe though, this time he should have a shake instead of a coke. If you're going to conjure, conjure boldly.

eleven

Ax Me No Sinners

"I don't care how venerable the tradition is," Pietro said as Madeleine turned up the gas under the broccoli. "I am not about to concede that the church has either the duty or the right to run clergy out on a rail just because they're sinners."

Madeleine sat down and challenged his point. "But even Scripture seems to say that the clergy have an obligation to set an example."

"Ah!" Pietro sighed, "First Timothy and all that. A bishop must be above reproach, temperate, sensible, no drunkard, keeping his children submissive and respectful in every way. An elder who persists in sin must be rebuked in the presence of all so that the rest may stand in fear."

"Well?"

"Well, what?"

"Oh, come off it," she huffed. "How do you square all that with your insistence that Jim Bakker shouldn't have gotten the ax?"

"Easy," Pietro said. "First Timothy says nothing against spending a night in a motel with a church secretary."

"Will you please be serious? You know perfectly well I agree with you. Why can't you just give me some answers that will convince those who don't?"

Pietro shook his head. "It's no use."

"Why?"

"Because, my Dear, Jim Bakker's sin was a sexual trespass. Once people get *that* bee into their bonnets, all other thoughts simply disappear."

Madeleine tried another tack. "Well then, forget about people in general and talk to me. I really would like to know what you think."

"Oh," Pietro said. "In that case . . ." He stood up and started pacing around the kitchen. "Point one. All that stuff in First Timothy and elsewhere is undeniably a good standard—and not just for the clergy but for everybody. But. But, but, but. Since the Gospel is about Christ dying for us while we were still sinners, the church has to be very careful not to give the impression that the standards should be turned into tests to be passed or failed. Otherwise, it shoots itself in the foot. We are saved by the cross and the resurrection, not by our behavior. But if you kick out a Jim Bakker for shacking up, you say in effect that that isn't the case. You say it's the absence of shacking up that saves, not the presence of Jesus."

"But . . ." Madeleine tried to interject.

"Let me say it for you so you don't slip back into speaking for people in general. I know what they say. They claim to believe that Jesus saves; but then they go on and act as if sin can still damn you—thus making sin more powerful than Jesus. Let me put it as plainly as possible. If there were no Jesus, Jim Bakker could avoid shacking up till all the cows in the universe came home and still not be saved. And if there is a Jesus, he is saved even if he hits every motel between here and Hong Kong."

"But only if he repents, right?" Madeleine shot in quickly.

"Wrong! That's hogwash on two counts. First of all, Jim Bakker is saved free for nothing by grace. He can repent and enjoy the grace that saves him, or he can not repent and not enjoy it. But whether he repents or not, the grace of God in Jesus is still there saving him. Repentance is not a work done antecedent to salvation; it's a response subsequent to a free and irrevocable gift of salvation already given. 'The gifts and the calling of God are without repentance'—if I may make a pun on Romans 11:29."

"What's the other count of hogwash?" she asked, ignoring the pun.

"The other count is that people who say, 'only if he repents,' don't mean a word of it—at least not when it comes to what they consider really sleazy sins. You want to know why I made that smart remark about First Timothy not mentioning clergy who bed church secretaries? Because while it omits that particular dereliction, it does include a definite condemnation of clergy who are 'lovers of money.'"

"What's that got to do with it?"

"Plenty. If people really think Jim Bakker can be saved only if he repents, they ought at least to have the decency to listen to the man's repentance. He *confessed* his fornication, for crying out loud! Why couldn't they just shut up and leave him to Jesus? The answer is that once they hear the word 'fornication,' they don't even remember he made a confession. All they really care about is behavior—and that's because what they actually believe is that it's behavior, and not Jesus, that saves."

"I still don't follow. Where does the part about being 'a lover of money' come in?"

"It proves my point. For every ten people who thought Jim Bakker should be kicked out for fornication, there had to be at least five who thought he lined his own pockets with too much PTL money—and who thought he should have repented of *that*, too. But so what? They already proved they didn't listen to repentances anyway. If he'd also confessed to avarice, they'd just have turned it into one more excuse for giving him the boot. They're not believers in forgiveness at all; they're just a bunch of scorekeeping moralists."

"And so?"

"And so as long as the church keeps running clergy off the farm for bad behavior, the world is going to go right on thinking that behavior is what God is really counting. All the church's talk about repentance will be seen as just a smokescreen for getting the goods on sinners—which is all the world has ever been interested in anyway, and which brings us, of course, to . . ."

Madeleine leapt up and lunged to turn off the gas as the broccoli boiled dry. "Oh, no," she said, as she ran water into the pot; "you weren't going to say 'Gary Hart,' were you?"

"Of course I was. You get an 'A'. He's the final demonstration. The secular order gave Gary Hart the ax; the ecclesiastical order gave Jim Bakker the ax. One might have hoped that there would have been a wee bit more grace and forgiveness in the second case than in the first, but there wasn't. *Ergo*, even the church is peddling bad news. Let's eat. This is even more depressing than burned broccoli."

twelve

Resurrecting Fannie Farmer

Pietro put a layer of tuna salad sandwiches into the buttered casserole, covered them with slices of cheddar cheese, added a second layer of sandwiches and drowned the whole with a seasoned egg and milk mixture. He was just about to slip the dish into the oven when Madeleine came into the kitchen.

"Not souffléed sandwiches again?" she wailed. "I know I agreed to your doing variations on themes for Lent, but I never expected you to stick to only two themes. Three weeks of soups followed by three weeks of bread custard is not penance, it's a punishment."

"Fear not, Love," he said soothingly. Just a few more days and you will rise to the smell of lamb roasting with rosemary and garlic. Not to mention wild rice, asparagus with hollandaise, braised endives, if I can find any, and whatever else your palate may pant for. Plus, of course, the 1974 Petite Sirah you've been slapping my hands away from since Christmas.

"It's not Easter day I'm worried about," she complained. It's the fact that it usually takes you at least another forty days to come off one of those variation kicks. I've seen you rummaging in *Fannie Farmer* lately. Confess. You've been dreaming up another series, haven't you?"

Pietro decided this was no time to broach the subject of his newest one-recipe-fits-all idea. Instead, he tried to placate her wrath over the present one.

"Now, now. Fannie hasn't failed us so far, has she? All I did was take her brilliant, if pretentiously named *Fondue Celestine* and carry it to heights and depths she left uncharted. She listed only lobster salad sandwiches as the foundation of the dish. One glance at the recipe, though, was all I needed to see that tuna, chicken, ham, beef, lamb, or pork salad would do just as well. You have been part of a journey of exploration."

"The trouble is," Madeleine said, "you never know when to stop. Meat salads are one thing. But peanut butter and bacon sandwiches in custard? I won't mention the two nights you tried to pass off macaroni salad and bean sandwiches on us."

"Brilliant ideas," Pietro said huffily, "are not vitiated by occasionally overreaching applications. Think of the medieval cathedrals. The flying buttress was the key to their construction; yet before it was perfected, there must have been many such buttresses that, as it were, crash landed. If there had been no one daring enough to persist with variations on the theme, we would have missed the glories of Chartres and Cologne. Just as you, my Dear, but for my willingness to attempt even macaroni sandwiches, might have missed the supreme dessert variation on *Fondue Celestine*: strawberry jam and almond paste sandwiches in a custard with Grand Marnier."

"Poppycock," she snorted. "There is absolutely no architectural parallel to what you do—unless you know of somebody who tried to make cathedrals out of baked beans."

Pietro felt he was getting nowhere, so he withdrew to his private thoughts. As usual, Madeleine had been right: he had indeed been toying mentally with an entirely new set of dishes made from a single recipe. Furthermore, he had been thinking of it as a kind of Eastertide tour de force.

The basic dish was a dessert—inexplicably omitted from the newest edition of *Fannie Farmer*—called Denver Chocolate Pudding. You made a simple flour, sugar, baking powder, and butter mixture as if for biscuits, added some cocoa and enough milk to make a thick batter, laced it with vanilla, spread it into a buttered baking dish, sprinkled the top with more cocoa and a mixture of white and brown sugars, and then poured over it a cup and a half of cold black coffee. When it was baked, the biscuit mixture rose to the top, the sugars formed a crust, and the coffee ran underneath to make a fudge sauce. Served with ice cream, it was simply spectacular.

He had made that for years as an emergency dessert, but it was not till one philosophical afternoon that its further possibilities had dawned on him. If you could pour liquid *on top of* biscuit mix and have it end up as a sauce on the bottom why, there was simply no end to what might be done. His first thought was to take out the cocoa, put in grated lemon rind, and then replace the black coffee with lemonade. Sure enough, it produced an equally stunning lemon cake floating on a lemon sauce. Thus emboldened, he tried a variation in which an orange-flavored batter was poured over sliced pineapple and the whole drowned in orange juice. Presto! Pineapple-orange Cake with orange sauce.

He had, in fact, made both of those as Sunday desserts during Lent; but now his mind was mulling over the even more fascinating prospect of pointing the recipe in the direction of a main dish. If you took the sugar out entirely—that is, if you used nothing more than a plain, fairly wet, drop-biscuit mixture and then poured a suitable liquid over it—what incredibly-sauced concoctions might you not produce?

To begin with, what about leftover cooked chicken in the bottom of the dish, seasoned ad lib (say, with curry, onion and apple), then covered with the batter, and submerged under a liquid composed of chicken stock and heavy cream? Or, what about the same, leaving out the curry and substituting raw oysters for the chicken—possibly with the seasonings for Pan Roast

Grand Central mixed in with the oysters: lemon juice, celery salt, paprika, Worcestershire, and butter?

Pietro could hardly wait for Lent to be over. His mind raced through ever-broadening avenues of exploration. Leftover diced ham mixed with a little prepared mustard on the bottom, batter in the middle—with perhaps some sliced Cheddar laid over it—and then the bath of stock and cream. Leftover roast beef on the bottom, and onion soup on top. Sautéed mushrooms and chopped spinach underneath with half-and-half over. Sliced hard-boiled eggs down with curried cream up. Or for that matter, dot the eggs with butter and anchovy paste, use plain cream, and . . . by George, he had just invented Scotch Woodcock Under Biscuits.

"What are you grinning about?" Madeleine asked. "When you sit there and say nothing, I get the creeps. I was right about the next forty days, wasn't I?"

"Only in the sense, my Love, that the people who watched the first flying buttress go up were right about the Cathedral of Notre Dame being as good as built. You are about to have the most amazing Easter season of your life, culinarily at least. You will celebrate the resurrection with dinners that actually rise—dishes that burst from the waters of their baptism, so to speak, with new and glorified bodies."

Madeleine shook her head. "I must say, you certainly don't shy away from flattering comparisons when it comes to your cooking. Isn't that just a tiny bit overweening?"

"Not at all," Pietro demurred. "I have never weened more modestly. None of the credit will go to me."

"Where will it go then?"

"To baking powder. But that's as much of the mystery as I'll disclose now; you've got to work your way through three more *Fondues Celestines* first. Just trust me: your Eastertide will be a gas indeed."

"If it involves beans," Madeleine began threateningly . . .

Pietro smiled inscrutably. "Faith, my Love, faith," he said. She threw a potholder at him.

thirteen

The Great Zucchini

"You'll never guess who's coming," Madeleine said as she hung up the phone. "That was Gina. They're up from Florida for a visit and they'll be here in an hour for brunch!"

"You're right," Pietro admitted, "I would never have guessed. Normally, before your sister and her crew get here, the grass withers and the holly goes into shock. Come to think of it, though, the cat's been practicing hiding under the bed for days. Nature knows."

"Oh, it's not all that bad."

"That's what the serpent said when he handed Eve the apple."

"C'mon. You like Harry, at least."

"True," Pietro said, "though 'marvel at' is nearer the mark. Your brother-in-law is the only man I know with two totally independent nervous systems. One belongs to an intelligent form of life, but the other is on loan from a giant zucchini. The way he stays sane is to shift over to the second one when his kids are around. Seriously, though. I'm supposed to feed and water those animals?"

"Don't worry about the kids," Madeleine said. "I can always run out and get cereal and milk for them. And we'll keep it simple for us: I've decided we're having omelets."

"Just omelets?" Pietro asked. Inwardly he was relieved, but he learned not to lower his left too quickly. "What kind?"

"Oh, you name some and I'll pick."

Pietro ran his mind's eye over the herb garden and the re-frigerator. "Parsley? Chive? Savory? Tarragon? Cheddar? Jarls-berg? Bacon?"

"That would be a nice one."

"That, my dear, was not one. That was seven. The goal in making omelets is to end up with a dish that tastes like egg plus something—not one that tastes like everything you can find pasted together with egg. Tell you what. You zip out and buy the monster munchies and I'll work on the human food. The only promise you have to make is to meet me back at the pass before they get here. There are some things even a grown man shouldn't be made to face alone."

She toddled off.

One omelet, indeed! Pietro snorted to himself. Why, he wondered, was the temptation to overuse seasonings and gar-nishes so great? Was it because American cooking had been bland for so long that once the breakthrough was made people saw nothing but an indiscriminate hole called "taste," into which anything could be dumped? And, from which nothing could ever be removed? That had to be the explanation for most of what passed for spaghetti sauce, for example. People's recipes for it seemed to grow like topsy. Every time a "new" seasoning came into their purview, into the mix it went, whether it made gastronomic sense or not. Nothing was thought through in terms of the basic ingredients. Instead, they aimed at the pro-duction of certain abstract "tastes."

"That's *Italian!*" the idiot in the TV commercial exclaimed; and all across America, there was not one who opened the mouth, or peeped—or even thought: "Italian *what?*" As a nation, we had gone from making mush of our raw ingredients straight over to the equal but opposite error of drowning them in stereotyped flavors. And all the while the bountiful offerings of the world's most fruited plain simply went begging.

We congratulate ourselves on our new-found love of International Food, Continental Cuisine and Ethnic Delights, as if the adjectives were the main matter and the foods involved, simply the modifiers. We raved so much about Sicilian eggplant, Middle-Eastern eggplant or Chinese eggplant, it hardly occurred to us any more that the culinary creative process should really begin by paying attention to eggplant.

"Sicilian," all too often meant cheap olive oil, burnt garlic and oregano; "Chinese," tired peanut oil, ginger and MSG. And "Middle Eastern" (depending on how many light-years away people's minds were from the uniquenesses of the actual Middle East) usually meant cinnamon, mint, lemon, dill, oregano, basil and cumin—all dumped into everything in the hope that the conjured up ghost of the region would absolve the cook's inattention to the food itself.

How, Pietro wondered, did such cooks think "ethnic" cuisines got started in the first place? Did they imagine the ancient Chinese suddenly getting a yen for "Chinese" food at the end of an all-night poker game and sending out for some? There wasn't anyplace open that early. They just had to sit down the way every other nation did and wonder what to do with all those eggplants.

Which meant, of course, not only keeping their eye on the eggplants rather than their ethnicity, but also being willing to come up with a lot of eminently forgettable dishes of eggplant.

It was that unwillingness to run the risk of failure, he supposed, that led so many cooks to over-season rather than use restraint. The inclusion of too many herbs, spices and oddments ensured at least that their products would taste like too many herbs, spices and oddments. They preferred that, apparently, to betraying their ignorance of how to enhance the basic food itself.

But ignorance was nothing to be ashamed of; it was a mountain to be climbed and gotten past. Right now, in fact, Pietro himself was in the throes of just such a challenge: Zucchini Soup. He had had innumerable recipes pressed upon him, but so far they were all soups that did little more than add zucchini to a preexisting flavor—usually that of commercial curry powder. Emphatic though they were, they emphatically did not taste anything like zucchini.

He had so far noted three things about zucchini. The first was that it was an excellent thickener for a soup, producing a fine puree without resort to grease, flour or eggs. The second was that it made a rich green color, and the third that it had the least pronounced flavor of all the squashes. The last two were the heart of the problem: the color prepared the mind for an intensity of taste that the substance itself could not deliver.

His best efforts so far (having forsworn curry, Worcestershire, tomato paste, cheese, hambones, etc.) had been a puree of zucchini boiled in chicken stock. He had seasoned it discreetly with nutmeg, lemon, salt and pepper, laced it liberally with heavy cream, and then garnished it with fine dice of actual zucchini. If people ate it with their eyes closed, they loved it; if not, their first comment was, "Oh, it's not *pea* soup?"

His reverie was interrupted by terrible shrieks from the driveway. They'd beaten Madeleine home! He was alone at the pass! On second thought, though, maybe it wasn't a total loss. He watched Harry emerge, ever so slowly from the car. Maybe the Great Zucchini himself could tell him something about soup. . . ."

fourteen

from the Woodshed

Pietro poured himself a cup of coffee and sat down across from Madeleine on the porch. "Behold," he said, "I am obedient to a fault: you command and I attend. Do I gather correctly that there is some large and earnest subject smoldering at the base of your brain?"

"It's not just *my* brain," she answered. "You have a problem. Every time you get emphatic about grace—about how everybody is forgiven in advance for everything, no matter how criminal or rotten—you get people furious. That Jim Bakker thing you did was only the latest example. *I* think you should at least try to reassure them that you're not advocating indifference to right and wrong."

"*You* think that? You, who have sat with me through my fits of apoplexy at Ronald Reagan's speeches? You, who have heard my fulminations against overcooked chicken breasts, against sopranos who flat, against sloppy workmanship wherever it rears its ugly head . . . ?"

"Don't *start!*" she said threateningly. You know perfectly

well that what they accuse you of is indifference to *moral* evil. And do me the favor of not saying that moral evils are just sloppy workmanship in the realm of human behavior. That's too intellectual. As far as they're concerned, moral evil is monstrous in a way that flat notes are not. You simply have to convince them that you *care*."

"Alas," Pietro sighed, lighting a cigar. "My life seems to be nothing but a succession of trips to the woodshed for taking Jesus and Paul seriously."

"I *said*, don't start! Just give them an answer. To make it easy for you, I'll ask their questions. All you have to do is respond."

"Hmmm," Pietro pondered. "Very well . . . ask away."

Madeleine marshaled her line of questioning briefly and began. "Does society have a right to punish criminals?"

"Yes; provided the punishment itself is not cruel and un-usual."

"Good," she said. "Question two. Do parents have an obligation to teach their children moral values and to enforce those values by suitable means?"

"That is questions two and three, actually," Pietro corrected her. But yes to both."

"Four," she said. "If you saw a crime being committed, would you try to stop it?"

Pietro hesitated a moment. "I imagine I would allow certain prudential considerations to influence my decision. Rash bravery is not my long suit. Still, within those limits, I think I would."

"I'll take that as a yes," she said. "Too many of those, though, and you'll sound as if you're simply trying to get off the hook by being affirmative. I want you to *explain* your case, not abandon it."

"I see your point," he admitted. "Maybe if you asked me some questions I could answer in the negative, I would do better."

"Fine. Question five. Would you hire a known child mo-lester as a baby sitter?"

"Emphatically not."

"Even though you believed him to be forgiven by Jesus?"

"I still would not. Prudence would dictate that I should not gamble someone else's safety on him, or her, unless I had reasonable assurance that her, or his, molesting days were over. And prudence, you will recall, is a moral virtue."

"I recall," she said. "But tell me, now. How do you reconcile such a nice, moral answer with what people see as the indifference to morality implied in your monomania for grace?"

"Simple," Pietro answered. "Grace in no way encourages indifference to moral considerations. Quietism (to give the monstrous proposition its proper name) is not an option for Christians. We may not sit idly by while evil goes about seeking whom it may devour. And the reason we may not has deep theological roots. The Word, the Second Person of the Trinity, who in Jesus took away the sins of the world by the grace of his death and resurrection, is the same Word who made the world to begin with. And when he gave his creatures their various natures, he indicated by that gift the precise qualities he loved about them: the chickenbreastness of chicken breasts, for example—or to come to the point, the elegant humanness of human beings. He made them to be themselves, not something else. Therefore he is against chicken breasts being turned into rubber and he is against human beings turning themselves into child molesters."

"But . . ." Madeleine interrupted.

Pietro cut her off. "Let me finish. Accordingly, when we engage in immoral behavior, we contradict the Word's word about us—and by the same token, we contradict our own nature, because only what he says about us can be the truth of our condition. Our immoral gainsayings are all, to one degree or another, just lies. Furthermore, since the Word came precisely to save—to restore, to make true again the creatures he made— he never goes back on the morality that is our beauty. On the cross, the Word is doing exactly and only what he did in creation—speaking our true nature into his Father's ear."

"But why does the cross look so much like just giving up and letting evil have its way?"

"Ah," Pietro said. "That is because the cross is directed not at moral evil but at Sin. Moral evil, we can often do something about—and when we have the power and the opportunity, we should do it with all the energy at our disposal. But *Sin*, which is the radical inability of human nature to be true to itself—our failure to bring off, individually or socially, a version of the world that actually squares with the Word's version of it—*that* hard fact of our existence we cannot undo just by willing to be better in the future. There is simply too much in the past that we cannot change. My parents, and my parents' parents' parents—and yours and everybody's, everywhere and always—have left us an intractable mess. And so have we with our own children. All our promises to do better tomorrow have given us only a today as unreformed as any yesterday. We still unspeak his word about us day in and night out. And those unspeakings, those contradictions, are irremovable from history by our efforts. Therefore, on the cross, the Word unspeaks our unspeakableness in the silence of his death and respeaks us into beauty by the power of his resurrection. He has made a new creation, you see. The only problem is, you can't see it, touch it, taste it, or smell it. You can only hear about it and decide to believe *him*. The opposite of Sin with a capital *S* is not morality; it's faith."

"So where does that 'unspeaking' leave morality?" Madeleine asked.

"Where it always was. It remains the truth about us, and it remains a truth that we forsake only at our own peril. In addition, it remains something that we should actively invite the world to conform itself to—precisely because, to whatever degree it does, it will become a place of beauty and joy. We do, after all, pray that God's will be done on earth as in heaven. But God is a realist, if nothing else: since total conformity to the moral law is something that has never shown any sign of arriving soon, God has decided not to count on it as a means for finally cleaning up the mess we have made. *While we were yet sinners*, Christ died for us. He has taken the cleanup entirely into his own hands. He has just gone and done it without waiting for us; and he invites us simply to trust that he has it all accomplished for us in Jesus—and to proclaim that trust by acting as if we really believed it."

"Can't you say it more succinctly?"

"Sure. The moral law is great stuff, but as an instrument of salvation, it's a bust."

"I didn't mean *that* succinctly."

Pietro took a long draw on his cigar. "All right. One more try. Take Auschwitz—the Holocaust. Auschwitz was immoral, yes. Further Auschwitzes should be prevented if possible, yes. But. The likelihood that all such inhuman horrors can be prevented by moral effort is the same for the future as it was for the past, namely, zero. Therefore when we have done all we can do to make the world right, we will still be left with a world that can be made right only by Someone with more moxie than we have."

"That wasn't succinct enough."

"True," Pietro conceded. But it wasn't too bad either—especially for someone in the woodshed."

fifteen

Held in Contempt

"Well!" Madeleine said, pouring her second cup of coffee with an aggressive hand. "You may like cocktail parties, but I can't stand them. How come you always waltz off and leave me to put up with the smallest talk in the room?"

Pietro had known since last evening that this conversation was brewing. Madeleine was by disposition and choice a one-on-one conversationalist. Large groups—especially peripatetic large groups—made her feel alienated from her environment. He cast about in his mind for a soft answer to turn away the barely submerged wrath. "I'm sorry about deserting you, Love," he began tentatively. "It's just that you seemed to be doing so well, babbling along with Suzanne. I figured you'd finally broken the disengagement syndrome."

"Well, next time just remember that I never do," she said flatly. "In fact, it was the conversation with Suzanne that made me furious. She's supposed to be one of my best friends, and there she was putting up a wall a foot thick between us."

The soft answer was not proving much of a success, but Pietro decided he was stuck with it. "It's just the nature of the beast," he said quietly. "Or more accurately, the beastly nature of the cocktail party. As an entertainment, the whole thing is a fraud. You walk in and it looks for all the world as if you've landed where the action is: beautiful people, gorgeously dressed, all chirping happily away. But when you actually try to get a piece of the action, what you find is that the person you're talking to has decided the real party must be somewhere else and is itching to get there: across the room, out on the porch— anywhere but where you happen to be standing. Suzanne was just going with the invidious flow."

Madeleine snorted. "It's invidious all right. And the flow is straight down the drain. A hundred and eighty degrees away from anything personal at all. How can you stand it?"

"I guess I just lower my expectations and let it happen," Pietro said. "Even so, the dreadfulness catches up with you. You know what I got as a penance for leaving you with Suzanne? Thirty minutes worth of being talked at, not to, about a variation of pesto that called for everything in the garden but Brussels sprouts. Not only that, but the self-proclaimed chef in question insisted on pronouncing it 'paste-o.' I thought I'd go out of my mind."

"Why'd you put up with it for half an hour then?" Madeleine asked.

"I didn't," Pietro said archly. "I politely tuned out the last twenty-five minutes of the show."

"Well then," Madeleine parried, "You're no better than Suzanne. You don't even care enough to insist on being talked to. At least I don't tune people out." She snatched up a copy of a Peter Wimsey mystery and ostentatiously began to read.

Pietro considered the maneuver for a moment and foolishly made the obvious comment. "But are you not, my Dear, doing just that right now?"

Menacingly, she slid her reading glasses down her nose and said, "No."

"What, then, would you call it?"

"I would call it giving you the full benefit of my personal anger. You are not being tuned out; you are being subjected to severe static. Bear it," she said, pushing the glasses back up, "like a man who is *in* instead of *out* of a relationship."

There are times when a man's only choice is to decide there is no choice. Pietro fell silent.

Madeleine, of course, was exasperating, but she had, as usual, struck home in the process of flailing about. Pietro was no exception to the rule that cocktail parties brought out the worst in people.

As he sipped his coffee in temporary exile, he realized that he was guilty of buying apparent virtue at the price of a rather large hidden vice. He could pride himself on an equanimity, a peaceableness of which Madeleine was incapable. He never clamored, never strove with people. But there was a catch in it. If he suffered fools gladly, he did so by the shabby device of writing them off as fools. He avoided anger by invoking contempt.

He had once heard a preacher who put forth the alarming proposition that certain human sins turned out to be virtues when practiced by God. Anger and jealousy were the only examples he could recall now—the point of the sermon escaped him completely. Still, if you followed it out a bit . . .

Being angry with people—even being jealous over them—was at least a way of saying you were still working on a relationship with them. And it said so even if you weren't God. But scorning people—disdaining them, despising them as not worth the bother of bothering—said only that you had given up on them completely. Even God, presumably, couldn't make a virtue out of that. No more then, Pietro decided, would he.

He congratulated himself on the resolution. With the enthusiasm of one who habitually assumed that a diagnosis did the work of a cure, he interrupted Madeleine's reading to report on his moral improvement.

She heard him out. Yes, he did tend to be subtly scornful. And yes, it was good of him to admit it. And yes indeed, it was a vice he could well do without—if and when he could manage between now and the next temptation to kick the habit of half a century.

But no, that particular reform was not what she had in mind at all. "What I had been hoping for," she said, removing the eloquent eyeframes and riveting him to the spot, "was a simple resolve not to desert me at cocktail parties."

Like Naaman the Syrian, when Elisha promised him a cure for his leprosy if he would simply wash himself in the river Jordan, Pietro felt that the treatment Madeleine proposed was a little short on spiritual glamor. Still a cure at the breakfast table was worth two in the future . . .

He rose and kissed her on the cheek. "To hear is to obey," he said. "I am your liege man of life and limb . . ."

"Will you cut that out," she exclaimed. "All I want is one human being I can talk to over the next batch of raw vegetables and cheap wine. Just say yes, for crying out loud."

"Yes," he said.

She kissed him.

sixteen

Angelique Bedeviled

Pietro followed Madeleine out of the kitchen. "You're not leaving me alone here with your cousin, are you?" he whispered, in barely controlled panic.

"Oh don't be silly," she said. "I'm only going to the Post Office. Besides, Angelique is practically a disciple of yours. She'll love watching you whip up something."

"She will not. Angelique is the original neat freak. Being around while I make *Leberkaese* is guaranteed to pop every circuit-breaker in her head."

Madeleine gave him an airy smile. "Better hers than mine. TTFN—Ta ta for now."

Pietro glared as she waved at him, and then he trudged back to the kitchen. Angelique was inspecting his spice rack—all thirty-one board feet of it. "How can you find *anything* here, Peter? I have mine all alphabetized."

He tapped his temple with a finger. "Memory, Love. I never have problems unless somebody makes the mistake of trying to organize me."

"Oh," she said, putting the thyme back next to the mar-joram again. "Well, at least I get a chance to watch the genius at work. What are you making?"

"*Leberkaese.*"

"What's that?"

"Liver loaf."

"Oh, goody, *pâté*. Lots of Cognac and garlic, I hope."

"Not a smitch of either, as a matter of fact. Nor is it ex-actly *pâté*, when you come right down to it. Actually, it's more of a cold cut. Just keep your eye on the bouncing ball, though, and we'll have a regular cookalong. Now then," he said, scratching his head, "if I recall correctly, I scribbled the recipe on the back of a LILCO envelope . . . Ah! there it is, sticking out of Jane Grigson's *The Art of Charcuterie*. Another triumph of culinary logic!"

He scanned the paper and began to assemble the ingredi-ents. "A pound of raw beef liver, a pound of raw pork, a half a pound of raw bacon, and a cup of chopped onion melted gently in a little lard. Let's take care of the onions first. Then I'll put the fine plate on the grinder and . . ."

"You're going to grind *raw liver?*" Angelique asked. "Yecch!"

"Yecch me no yecchs. When I was a tiny tot, I was fed ground raw liver every day—with stewed tomatoes mushed into it for good measure."

"How awful! You must have been raised by barbarians."

"Not at all. My mother, wanting nothing but the best for me, took me to a Park Avenue pediatrician who decided that I needed iron in my diet."

"Why didn't he prescribe capsules or something?"

"That was not possible. You must understand that when I was a tad, such pharmaceutical breakthroughs had not yet oc-curred. In fact, the waters of the Flood had just barely begun to recede. Actually, though, I found my daily dish of raw liver as palatable as it was memorable."

"I'd die before I'd eat it. And I don't think I could stand grinding it up, either."

Pietro cut all the meats into strips and started the machine. "I'd suggest a respectful distance then," he advised. "This is not always a tidy operation." He held a piece of liver over the feed tube and waited for her to move.

"Oh, just go ahead. I'll cover my eyes."

"As you like, my Dear," he said, dropping the liver into the tube. It squirted energetically out of the faceplate, landing mostly, but not quite entirely, in the bowl.

"You got it on my skirt!" Angelique screamed. "If you'd break down and buy a food processor, things like this wouldn't happen."

"True," he observed quietly—but then thought to himself: If you'd backed off like I told you, Sweetheart, you wouldn't be carrying on like it was World War III.

All he said, however, was, "Sorry about that, Angelique. Use a little cold water. It'll come out."

By the time she finished her cleanup, Pietro had ground both the meat and the onions three times. He paused to inspect the damage to Angelique's skirt. There was no liver spot, but it now sported a water stain the size of a skillet. "Very good," he said. "You did a nice job on the surrounding area, too."

She sniffed and sat down on the other side of the room. "Well, I guess it'll be all right. What's next?"

"Simplicity itself. We dissolve four packages of gelatin in a cup of cold chicken stock, heat it up, and then run the ground mixture through a blender in three batches—adding one egg and a third of the stock to each batch."

Pietro put an egg and some stock into the blender and added the first installment of the meat mixture. A certain amount ran down the outside of the machine and onto the counter.

"Really, Peter! Can't you even *try* to be neat? Uggh!"

71

"Patience, patience," he cooed, emptying the first batch into a clean bowl. "The worst will be over in a minute."

She stared out the window till he was done. "By the way," she asked, "what kind of gelatin did you put in? Lemon?"

Pietro shrieked inwardly, but limited himself to the words, "No. Plain," spoken through clenched teeth.

"Oh. Well. Is it all done now?"

"No, it gets a cup of sifted fine white bread crumbs, a good two teaspoons of salt, and a little under a tablespoon of *quatre épices*.

"What's that?"

The *charcutier's* magic ingredient: seven parts black pepper, and one part each of nutmeg, cloves, and cinnamon, all ground up fine. After that's in, all we have to do is beat the mixture thoroughly, grease a loaf pan, fill it up, and bake it at 325 degrees for an hour and a half—in a pan of hot water, of course. But lo!" he interrupted himself brightly, "the mistress of the house approacheth. You are delivered from any further assault on either your sensibilities or your wardrobe."

"What a mess!" Madeleine exclaimed from the doorway. "C'mon into the living room, Angelique, and we'll have a glass of . . . Good Lord! What happened to your skirt?"

Pietro did a fast pivot, fetched the jug of wine, and pressed it into Madeleine's hands. "There, there. Least said, soonest mended, you know. I'm sure you'd love to keep me company while I tidy up, but in the words of an old friend of mine, a hearty TTFN to you both."

seventeen

Angelique Diabolique

"You've simply *got* to give me the recipe for the *sauce* you put on that *fish*," Angelique burbled across the dining room table. "It was absolutely *fab*."

Pietro hated people who talked in italics, he despised the word *fab*, and he put no faith whatsoever in the attention span of Madeleine's cousin. "Oh," he said, trying to fob her off, "it's hardly a recipe, just a trick . . ."

Madeleine shot him a glance. Only this morning she'd lectured him on what she called his congenital snobbery—his habit of putting people off because he'd decided they didn't really want the information they asked for. Her look said, "respond in full, or else!"

Pietro reversed field in mid-fob: ". . . but now that I think of it, Angelique, maybe after I tell you the trick, I actually will give you a recipe. How's that?"

"That's *wonderful*, Peter. Just let me get my cigarettes from the living room. I don't want to miss a *word*."

He looked for an approving nod from Madeleine, but she'd

begun clearing the table. You'd think, he thought to himself, that when people expected you to do the impossible they could at least not disappear into the kitchen while you . . .

"I'm *back!*" Angelique proclaimed, settling herself. "Now! Tell me *all!*"

Pietro tried to get it over with quickly. "The trick is, after you've sautéed the fillets, you deglaze the pan with a wine-based fish stock, then . . ."

"Not so fast," Angelique interrupted. "*First,* what were the fish coated with?"

"Flour. Lightly. Then a little egg."

"Could I use crumbs?" she asked.

"When?" he countered. "In place of the flour or after the egg?"

"I don't know," she said blithely. "When *should* I use them?"

Pietro thought briefly of explaining that it could only be after, otherwise the egg would wash the crumbs off. He mastered the temptation, however. With Angelique, one explanation always led to another subject.

"You shouldn't use them at all," he said flatly.

"But I *like* crumbs."

"You also liked *my* fish. And on *that,* I used only *flour* and *egg.*" He swallowed hard. He realized he was speaking in italics too.

"Oh. Well. Fine," she chirped. "*Now!* Tell me what you sautéed them in."

"Butter."

"Could I use margarine?"

"No," he said, trying to avoid another explanation.

"Why not?"

Pietro felt a flash of heat across the base of his skull. He gripped the arms of his chair and forced himself to smile. "Heh, heh. Because then you wouldn't be making my recipe, would you, my Dear?"

Angelique looked at him as blankly as if he had just spoken Swahili. She went straight on: *"Next,* I need to know what *deglaze* means."

"It means you take the fish out of the pan, then add liquid and boil it down, stirring all the while to loosen any goodness that's stuck to the bottom. At the end, you could add some capers, swirl in some butter, check it for salt and/or lemon and pour it over the fish. Simple, right?"

"I guess so," she said distractedly. "But before you go any further, could you be a love and get me another glass of wine? Talking about food always makes me thirsty."

He obeyed, glad for the respite. He also fetched a pad and pencil in the hope of eliminating at least one more interruption.

"For writing down the recipe," he said, as he pushed them toward her.

"Oh, thanks. But I don't need them. Just tell me how you make the fish stock."

Pietro decided that speed would be his only salvation: "You take one carrot, one onion, one celery rib, one handful of parsley, a pinch of thyme, a blade of mace, a half a clove, six white peppercorns, a pinch of salt, and the bones from the fish and you put them in a pot and cover them with half dry white wine and half water and boil them for ten minutes or so then you strain off the stock and use that to deglaze the . . ."

"I never have fish bones," she said.

"Then throw in some trimmings off the fillets."

"Suppose they're already too small?"

"Go out and buy some extra fillets."

"What if the store is closed?"

"Make it without fish, then. Listen Angelique, are you sure you don't just want to dump a can of mushroom soup on some fish sticks? I mean . . ."

"Well! You don't have to get huffy with me, Peter. Just because not everybody is a natural cook like you . . ."

Madeleine returned from the kitchen as her cousin marched down the hall. "Well," she said to Pietro, "at least you *tried* to respond. Don't you feel better?"

"No," he snapped. "Trying does no good at all. It's not what we do that people find unpardonable; it's who we are. I'm a congenital snob and Angelique's a congenital twit. The miracle is that anybody puts up with anybody. How do *you* manage it, by the way? What's the secret, love or something?"

"It's love or nothing. I just decided a long time ago to pardon who you are."

"Lucky for me. But isn't that hard?"

"Sometimes. There's a bonus, though."

"What?"

"Pardoning who you are guarantees I always have you around. That way, I never have to stop complaining about what you do."

"That's a bonus?"

"Are you kidding? For a congenital nag like me, it's practically a godsend."

eighteen

Mr. Ewing Goes to Washington

"Presidential campaign, my eye," Madeleine huffed. "All we're getting is reruns of *Dallas*. First it was Gary Hart and some blonde. Then it was Senator Biden with his book of quotations too loose in the holster. Then it was Judge Ginsburg and pot. All the press hands us is peccadilloes, not political analysis. The Europeans are right: America acts as if it's canonizing saints, not picking someone who might be able to run a government."

Pietro, unwisely, tried his old balancing act. "On the other hand," he said between puffs on his pipe, "at least some members of the press have been critical of the fraternity's scandal-mongering. Tom Wicker, for example, in today's *Times*, . . ."

"Oh, come off it," Madeleine snapped. "That proves only that Tom Wicker has tenure or something. Sure, they print a handful of tsk-tsk pieces against themselves, but they keep right on scratching the American itch for cheap shots and tacky news. And why? Because they know that, deep down, we'd rather think about J. R. than about real life."

"Hmmm," Pietro said. "It suddenly occurs to me that you

may be on to something there. Maybe we're not as bad as we think."

"Well, it sounds pretty bad to me. J. R. will bed anybody to make a buck and kneecap anybody who gets in his way, and we lap it up. But when we pick a President, we pretend to be looking for Little Lord Fauntleroy. You know what I think that means? I think it means the whole country is schizophrenic."

"I don't think it means that at all," Pietro said calmly. "What occurred to me is that, for all his sleaze, J. R. is the only character in the show who has what a politician is supposed to have, namely, purpose. All the rest of the motley crew are foundering in the wake of each other's fecklessness. So the fact that the American public cheers for J. R., and yawns every time Bobby, Jenna, Ray, or Miss Ellie come on the screen, just might mean we can still recognize a politician when we see one."

"Hey, whoa!" Madeleine protested. "I didn't mean to divorce politics and morality *that* completely. Keep that up, and you could justify Hitler."

Pietro allowed himself a small, satisfied smile. "Not at all," he said. "There is indeed a place for moral judgments in politics; but the moral judgments need to be made first of all on the politicians' purposes and policies, not on their occasional bedroom practices or their history of puffing at college parties."

"But isn't there at least *some* connection between ethical public policies and private moral practices?"

"Not nearly enough," Pietro said, "to warrant the U-turn you seem to have executed on your original complaint about the press's moral nit-picking. Let me illustrate. Take Hitler. At this moment, I don't really know beans about his private morality—maybe he was more of a stinker than J. R., maybe less. But since his public purposes were monstrously immoral, I take the view that he should have been condemned even if he led the domestic life of an English country parson. Always remember, you don't need bad people to get bad deeds done. All you need is

somebody clever enough to convince good people that a nefar-
ious policy is actually the greatest thing since the pop-up
toaster. As I have frequently observed, most of the serious evils
in the world have been done in the name of good."

"But is there really no connection . . . ?"

"My Dear, my Dear," Pietro said, looking solicitous. "Are
you quite sure you are the same sharer of my bed and board
who began this conversation? Or has the schizophrenia that you
castigated in the country at large crept into your own soul?"

"Okay, okay," Madeleine said exasperatedly. "So I'm arguing against myself. So I don't worship at your altar of consis-
tency. So what? I asked you a question; just give me an answer,
not a lot of psychobabble."

"Very well," Pietro replied. "This much connection I'll give
you: if a politician's private faults are such that they will impede
either his own high purposes or those of the body politic over
which he presides, then he should be shunned. We do not need
a President who is blind-staggering drunk by 10:00 a.m. every
day, or one who has the liar's habit of telling people what he
thinks they want to hear. But please note that those two sample
faults are not possessed by J. R. Ewing in any way. J. R., for all
his tippling, is never drunk; and J. R. is never so wishy-washy as
to tell people simply what they want to hear. He invariably tells
them what *he* wants them to hear—though, like a good politician, he is wonderfully aware of how their desire to hear certain
things can be made to serve his purposes."

"But . . ."

"But," Pietro went blandly on, "since J. R.'s boudoir tactics
(to name only his saltiest fault) do not, in the context of the series, interfere in any material way with the prosecution of his
purposes, I judge that they must be considered immaterial—as
should any politician's faults of similarly minor character."

"What about Gary Hart?"

"Ah!" said Pietro. "I think I lack sufficient information

about the gentleman to give you a concrete answer. But in the abstract, it is certainly possible that a person's sexual escapades might amount to a fault that was not so minor. Coupled as such shenanigans could be with a deep and disturbing belief in his own invisibility, they might constitute a warning sign to a prudent electorate. But of course, the crippling fault would then lie in the area of self-knowledge, not simply between the sheets."

"You realize, don't you, that your position on this will strike the *Door*'s readers as somewhat out of line with truth, justice, and the American Way—not to mention the Bible?"

"No doubt," Pietro answered. "For their comfort, therefore, I shall bolster my conviction with Scripture. It seems to me that in a world populated entirely by sinners (Galatians 3:22), it is simply idle to hope that a presidential candidate will turn out to have been Saint Superman for even twenty minutes, let alone for the entirety of his life. We are looking for a politician with moral purposes, not for a savior with moral perfection. Besides, if you will recall, even the true Savior was not generally admired for his saintliness—and when he actually did his saving, he did the job as Clark Kent, not Superman."

"But wasn't Jesus totally moral?"

"So the church encourages us to think, and so I encourage myself to believe. To give him credit, though, plenty of people thought he was a very bad person."

"As bad as J. R.?"

"Worse," Pietro said. "After all, J. R. hasn't yet been bad enough to get himself crucified."

"Where does all this come out? You think you might run J. R. for president?"

Pietro smiled. "It has happened before and we're still here to talk about it. On balance, though, I suspend judgment. Until I have heard his—or anyone else's—purposes for the country, I am not about to be alarmed by reports that he is a sinner. *That*, after all, we knew already.

nineteen

Thirty-two Pounds of Pork

Pietro surveyed the totally empty meat market and congratulated himself on yet another triumph of his theories about the time to shop. Householders, he maintained, fell into two categories: the anticipators who bought their meat in the morning; and the procrastinators who waited till late afternoon. At either of those times, it was practically a certainty that the "Now Serving" number on the wall of the shop would be a good twenty numbers below the one on the paper tongue the butcher's dispenser stuck out at him. If, however, he shopped between three and three-thirty, there was a good chance that all the meat buyers, provident or not, would be home waiting for school buses. He surreptitiously stuck out his own tongue at the dispenser and bellied up to the counter.

"Loins of pork," he said, broaching the subject of his quest. "Still eighty-nine cents a pound?" Getting the nod, he asked John the butcher for the biggest one in the store. The ad had claimed they were running from sixteen to twenty-four pounds; he was hoping he could spring for top weight.

81

"You really mean the biggest?" the butcher asked with mischief in his eye. "Hold on. We just got in a new shipment."

He came back bearing the largest single piece of pork Pietro had seen in years. "Got to be over thirty pounds", John said. "I'd hate to get caught between a wall and the hog this one came off. You still serious?"

"Absolutely," Pietro beamed. "The very thing I've been looking for. I have a friend who says I'm so bowlegged, I couldn't stop a pig in a ditch. Nobody could be too bowlegged for that one."

"How do you want it cut up?" John asked, ignoring the banter.

Pietro thought for a moment. "Hardly at all," he said. "Just take out the fillet, saw off the chine and cut the whole thing in three: one-fourth off the rib end, one-fourth off the loin end, and leave the half in the middle alone. I'll do the rest myself."

John shrugged and went to work. The fillet came out like the tenderloin from a small steer. The loin was then cut in three, weighed with the fillet, and hefted over to the bandsaw to remove the ridge of backbone along its length.

"I'll take those bones, too," Pietro called out over the noise, just in time to rescue them from the scrap bin. "All the more for the stock pot."

"You sure you don't want anything more done with this?" John asked. "Pretty fatty."

"So much the better for the sausage," Pietro said. "I like at least one-fourth fat; otherwise it's too dry. What was the total weight by the way?"

"Thirty-two," the answer came. "$28.48 altogether. Anything else?"

"Nope, that cleans me out. The trick now is to go home and make it worth twice that."

Madeleine was on her way out when Pietro staggered in with the two bags. "What on earth did you buy?" she asked, shaking her head. "Half interest in a pig farm? I hope you have all that disposed of before I get back. On second thought, I'll call and check before I come home. I signed on for a marriage, not a job in a meat-packing plant."

She marched to the car without a backward look and Pietro went to work. First he boned out the center section, trimmed it (tossing the scraps into a giant bowl), and then cut it into one large roast, one small one, and some three-quarter pound chunks for Chinese dishes. He cradled the roasts into sections of reversed rib bone, then tied and wrapped them. The chunks went, separately wrapped, into a plastic bag. With part of the operation completed, he lugged the results out to the freezer.

Next, he took a twenty-quart pot, tossed in the bones already on hand, and added to them the ones he then boned out of the ends of the loin. He carried the pot to the sink, pressed down the bones with the flat of his hand, filled the pot with water up to his wrist-bone and set it on the stove over a slow fire. After a couple of hours, it would get vegetables and seasonings. Right now though, it was time for sausage.

He cut all the remaining meat and fat into pieces the grinder would accept and ran everything through the coarsest blade once. He then put the meat into three separate bowls and consulted his recipes.

Breakfast sausage. For each pound of ground pork: 1 tsp. salt, ½ tsp. black pepper, ½ tsp. sage and a pinch of red pepper. Pietro figured the weight of meat in the first bowl and then overdid everything but the salt. He did not like unemphatic sausage.

Sweet Italian sausage. For each pound: 1 tsp. salt, ½ tsp. black pepper, 1 Tbs. fennel seed. In the second bowl, he overdid only the black pepper: the fennel struck him as already more than enough.

The third bowlfull he seasoned for *chorizo,* or *Spanish sausage.* Per pound: 1 tsp. salt, ½ tsp. black pepper, ½ tsp. ground coriander seed, 1 tsp. oregano, 1 Tbs. paprika, 1 clove garlic, crushed, generous pinches each of cumin and red pepper, 1 Tbs. vinegar, 2 Tbs. water. Here, he overdid everything, salt included. *Chorizo* was his favorite.

He then mixed the meat and seasonings in each of the three bowls, one after another (adding a bit of water to the first two as well). Finally, he put them (in the same order) through the coarse blade once more and again blended the contents of each bowl with his hands.

Pietro had sausage casings tucked away in the freezer, but with nearly eighteen pounds of sausage meat and Madeleine's resignation on his hands, he was not about to let himself in for the bother of stuffing them. Instead, he wrapped his products in bulk according to his latest system.

The breakfast sausage, he packed into plastic sandwich bags to be frozen and then collected into one large bag. When he wanted sausage to serve with eggs, all he had to do was quarter the packages and fry the resultant square patties. His mnemonic for recognizing these in the freezer was: Sausage à la White Castle Hamburgers.

The Italian sausage, he formed into 1 pound rolls in plastic wrap. These he kept in mind as sausage à la Karl Ehmer's Braunschweiger. Half-thawed, they sliced nicely into rounds.

The *chorizo* he froze as flat slabs in large plastic bags—to be remembered as Sausage à la Roofing Slate. The beauty of the three different shapes was that he never had to bother labeling anything: instant identification by sight alone.

He had just put it all in the freezer when Madeleine phoned to see if the coast was clear.

"Not only clear, my Love; if you don't get back here in short order, you'll find it desolate. I'm frying up a sample of *chorizo* and opening myself a beer. As I judge, I'll be sitting down to a snack in five minutes. Don't say I didn't give you fair warn . . ."

Madeleine hung up abruptly. She made it home in under four.

twenty

Banishing the Blues
With a Red Sauce

"Nothing but the oil bill and another catalogue from Frederick's of Hollywood," Pietro growled as he poked the day's mail between the flour and sugar canisters. "And the box rent had the nerve to be due. The Postal Service employees did their usual eye-rolling over my taste in reading matter. For this I pay the government?"

He had not quite forgiven Madeleine her most recent birthday joke on him. Last year's subscription to *Playboy* could always be explained away by saying he liked to keep up with Hugh Hefner's theology. But the Frederick's catalogue? This was the third issue so far and he had yet to think of an explanation that didn't make him sound like a victim of testosterone poisoning.

"Cheer up," she said. "I'd rather have a dirty old man than none at all. Besides, Angelo came by while you were out and dropped off some fish."

Pietro's mood brightened. "What kind?"

"Blues, I think."

"And when caught?"

"He didn't say, but I got the impression it was early this morning. Why?"

"Angelo's generosity sometimes exceeds his honesty. He may fish every morning, but he's not above giving away yesterday's catch so he can keep today's for himself. Do you recall the potfull of vintage flounders he delivered two weeks ago?"

"They weren't that bad," she remonstrated. "You should be grateful. If it were up to you we'd never lay eyes on fish. And after all, you're the cook who says that even sneaker tongues can be served if you make the right sauce."

He said no more and headed for the refrigerator. He was indeed a cook, and he was even more definitely no fisherman at all. He jinxed every trip he was on. Angelo had taken him only once—and quickly promised to keep him supplied all summer, just as long as he would keep his feet on dry land.

Still, that one trip had made him chary about freshness, and he tried to put the lone fish they caught that day in the cooler. Angelo yanked it out and dropped it in a bucket of water that would have warmed the heart of a solar energy buff. In Angelo's view of the universe the first and great commandment was, "Thou shalt let nothing warm the beer."

Pietro emptied the sack of fish into the sink. They had been cleaned, but the heading and gutting had been done in the slapdash fashion he had come to know and hate. Why couldn't fishermen be trained to take some pains with the job? And if they had to do it at all, why didn't they scale them before they took the heads off? Oh, well. He would simply fillet and skin them and settle for a pan-fried presentation with butter and lemon.

First, though, the all-important test. He rinsed one fish thoroughly in cold water and sniffed it critically. As he thought. If this fish was caught this morning, Pietro was still a college freshman. It had seen, by his reckoning, at least two sunrises from the wrong side of the waves and it might even, with Angelo's handling, have gotten sun poisoning as well. He canceled the idea of a simple presentation. This fish was going to need a full disguise.

Still, one shouldn't complain. Free fish was the only fish he ever cooked anymore. The markets had priced the finny creatures up to the skies; and as far as crustacea were concerned . . . why it took a bank loan to spring for shrimp, even if you settled for inconsiderable 21-25's. And lobster? If he recalled correctly, the last one that made a house call had come at a fee that would have elated a brain surgeon.

Seafood, in Pietro's household, now consisted chiefly of what you could catch with a can opener. Anchovies, sardines, kippers and, of course, the fish-of-all-work, tuna. Well, not even tuna, to tell the truth. About a year ago, he had taken to buying canned jack mackerel. Properly prepared—with good mayonnaise, lots of celery, a hint of onion and a heavy hand with the red pepper sauce—it made a tuna salad that would fool even the fussiest teenage palate. His children still didn't know, but he had cut the tunafish sandwich item in the household budget by half.

He brought himself back, however, to the fish at hand. There were four fifteen-inch blues. He boned and skinned them with a Chinese cleaver and whacked them into serving-size pieces. Now though, how to cook them? Some people made the mistake of cooking over-the-hill fish to mush. They had a vain hope that excess might cure what defect had caused; but that was not Pietro's way. For him, overcooked fish was like well-done beef: a federal crime. He would roll the pieces in a light coating of peppered crumbs and fry them quickly in very hot olive oil.

But the sauce, the all-important mask without which this meal could be no ball at all: what would it be? He thought for a moment and went to work.

The water went on for the pasta. When it boiled, he dropped in eight ripe tomatoes from the garden, gave them a minute or so, fetched them out with a slotted spoon and peeled off the skins. Then he put them on the cutting board, chopped them up coarse, tossed them into a waiting pot and put them over high heat.

Meanwhile, he put a coating of olive oil into a saucepan, chopped up an onion and a couple of garlic cloves, and set them to simmer. After the tomatoes had boiled for a minute he put a strainer over the onion/garlic/oil saucepan and drained the juice into it, leaving the tomatoes behind in the original pot. Then he squeezed half a lemon into the strainer, removed it to the sink and set the juice boiling hard to reduce it.

The sauce would still not be emphatic enough, so he sent a passing child out into the garden to cut a small bowlfull of tarragon. Half of that, chopped up, would go into the saucepan now; the other half, in long leaves, would be added fresh at the last minute.

After that, it was all plain sailing, even if it had not started out as great fishing. A salad would be a nice touch, but someone else would have to fix the greens. Putting on his best macho voice, he shouted to Madeleine to get into something diaphanous from Mr. Frederick's and let herself be dominated for ten minutes while he minded the pasta, fried the fish, and removed the fillets to a platter. That done, he deglazed the frying pan with about half of the tomato reduction, added some chopped tomato from the pot, stirred it all up with a large lump of butter, checked the seasoning and poured it over the fillets. The rest of the juice, plus another lump of butter, went back into the pot of chopped tomatoes along with salt and pepper.

"What, by the way," Madeleine asked, "is the name of this dish you're serving with my salad?"

"It's called *Pesce, Ballo in Maschera*, wench. I got the idea from that girl with the rhinestone mask on page four of the catalogue. In any case though, I have finished. It goes out with the linguine and the fresh tomato sauce. While you serve it, I shall take my place at the head of the table and await my wine. And by the way. Don't forget the fresh tarragon. Like the rest of us, that fish needs all the help it can get."

twenty-one

The Short and Long of It

"Where do they get off with this blasphemy?" Madeleine fumed, throwing down the newspaper. "I'm sick and tired of TV preachers who blather on about AIDS being the 'scourge of God' on homosexuals and drug users. If they're going to destroy the Good News like that, they should be forbidden to call themselves evangelists. Right?"

Pietro relit the ashes in his pipe, stalling for time.

"Well?" she snapped.

"I think I shall refuse to answer on the grounds that it might tend to incinerate me."

"Bad puns make me even more furious than Bad News. Give me an answer or I'll reduce you to less of an ash than you've got in that silly pipe. And take it out of your mouth when you talk. It makes you mumble."

"Ah," Pietro said, putting down the pipe. "The question, I take it, is whether I think AIDS is the scourge of God. Would you like the short answer or the long one?"

"Short, please."

"Very well. The answer is no."

Madeleine made the mistake of rising to the bait. "Is that all you have to say?"

"Of course not," Pietro said. But you chose the short answer."

"Well, can't you make it a *little* longer?"

Pietro smiled ingratiatingly. "Anything to please a steady customer. Listen closely, though, or you'll miss it: God, as he reveals himself in Jesus, deals with the world by grace and forgiveness, not by dunning and foreclosure, let alone by getting even."

"That's *all?*" she huffed.

"No," he said blandly. "But when the customer says 'short', I try to be the soul of concision. For me to say more would require another choice on your part."

"What choice?" Madeleine asked.

Pietro smiled his shopkeeper's smile again. "You have to decide whether you want an answer with distinctions or without."

"What is this with you today? You're harder to get started than an old car at forty below."

Pietro just kept smiling and repeated himself: "With or without distinctions, Madam?"

"Oh, all right," she said. "With, I guess."

"An excellent choice. In that case, the answer is yes and no."

"Will you *stop!*" Madeleine raged. "Say something substantive, for heaven's sake!"

Pietro picked up his pipe and ostentatiously put it down again. "This conversation reminds me of an old cheese store owner I used to deal with. I went into his shop one day to buy some of that Turkish sesame-seed confection—halvah. I asked for a pound; but rather than reach for the halvah, he simply looked at me and asked, 'Vanilla or chocolate'? I thought for a second and said, 'Vanilla'. Without batting an eye, he asked, 'Marbled or plain?' I thought again and said, 'Marbled'. Going right on, he asked, 'With nuts or without?' But before I could get even a word of my exasperation out, he said, 'You think it's easy to come in here and buy halvah?' I feel very much, my dear, as if I am in that man's shoes."

Madeleine glowered at him. "Okay, okay," she said. "Give

me a pound of anything you've got, as long as it's not just hot air."

"Do I take it that Madam has now opted for the slightly longer version of the answer, *with* distinctions?"

"Yes, yes. Just get on with it."

Pietro refilled his pipe, but kept it in his hand. "Well, in the sense that AIDS is caused by a virus that is one of God's creatures, AIDS is something which God, at the very least, *allows* to happen. Furthermore, insofar as AIDS, in many cases, afflicts persons whose sexual or drug-related behavior has, at times and by some, been held to be contrary to God's will, we might even be tempted to say that since the virus was contracted as a result of such behavior, that consequence itself was allowed by God. Accordingly, in some large, loose, and mostly rhetorical sense, we might also be led to call it a scourge of God—much as Attila the Hun was called the scourge of God on ancient Rome, or as the confusion of tongues at the Tower of Babel could be seen as the scourge of God on human pride."

Madeleine looked shocked. "You're saying AIDS *is* the scourge of God?"

"Not at all. That was merely the first half of my distinction. Allow me to continue with a very large *however*." Pietro became earnest. "However," he said, "in the fullness of the revelation of God in Christ, we get a different picture. Jesus came not to judge the world but to save it. Therefore, if God has a program for dealing with the world's sins, *in the here and now*—which is precisely the frame of reference of all this talk about AIDS as the scourge of God—his program cannot possibly involve his using AIDS as a tit-for-tat retaliation for human behavior. God's program is grace, not scorekeeping; free gift, not reward and punishment in this world. Accordingly, under this second half of my distinction, AIDS is emphatically *not* the scourge of God."

"Why do you have to make it so complicated?" Madeleine asked.

Pietro smiled again. "If Madam will cast her mind back, she did ask for the marbled halvah. But to continue. The case against

AIDS being the scourge of God can be proved not only by the Gospel but by simple justice and logic. Not everyone who gets the affliction is guilty of debatable behavior. A dutiful wife can contract it from her husband. An unborn fetus can inherit it from its mother. An innocent recipient of contaminated blood can even pick it up in a hospital. *Ergo*, in the final analysis, being afflicted with the disease has no necessary connection with morality."

"Well," Madeleine said, I'm glad you finally came down on the right side—I think."

"Thank you," Pietro said. "But Madam's purchase is not yet complete."

"What's left?"

"The choice between with nuts or without."

Madeleine looked confused. "Another choice?"

"Actually, no," Pietro reassured her. "By asking your original question in terms of TV evangelists, you already opted for *with* nuts. Those types are simply goofy when it comes to the Gospel. They're preaching law, not grace—and they're doing it almost two thousand years after Paul, in the Epistle to the Romans, proved that law cannot possibly be an instrument of salvation. Oh, sure, the law is holy, just, good, and all that. But since nobody can keep it, God refuses to use it as a test of anybody's acceptability. He simply accepts us all in the Beloved and asks us to trust that free gift."

"Aren't you going to name any of those evangelists? It would serve them right."

Pietro finally lit his pipe. "Oh, no. As the old lady in Maine said when she was asked who her favorite among the presidential candidates was, 'I never mention their names. It only encourages them.'"

"You know something? I can't remember when you've been *this* impossible on a subject."

Pietro puffed out a large cloud of smoke. "You think it's easy to come in here and ask a question about the scourge of God?"

twenty - two

Carlo the Crass

Madeleine waited until they were a safe distance from their hosts' door. "What an evening!" she whispered into Pietro's ear. "There's only one thing worse than having to sit through a defense of vegetarianism and that's listening to attacks on it from rude people. If Melanie and Morris want to live on bulghur wheat and lemon juice, okay; but why do they invite guests they know are going to hassle them about it? Who was that boor, anyway?"

"I presume," Pietro said, once they were inside the car, "that you're talking about Carlo the Carnivore, the east coast's world-class vegetarian-baiter."

"I certainly am," Madeleine huffed. "How does he get the nerve to insult his hosts like that—carrying on deliberately about the joys of butchering deer? Can't he see it offends them?"

"You have to understand something about types like Carlo, my Love," Pietro said. "He may delight in meat, but his favorite dish is a tender conscience. He just likes to shock people. He probably thinks that's the way to convert them."

"Well, it isn't. Of all the idiotic conversations . . . at the end, it sounded as if the world's options on the subject of food boiled down to either raw venison or brown rice cooked to glue. How come you didn't try to say something at least reasonable?"

Pietro started the car and gave a philosophical wave of his hand. "I never interfere in theological arguments between zealots. It's against my religion."

"Which is?" Madeleine asked.

"Devout Cowardice," Pietro answered. "Seriously, though, once a discussion degenerates into berating people for their beliefs, there's no point trying to get intelligence back into it. I just opt out."

"You mean you opt in: to the nearest wine jug. You want me to drive?"

"Now that you mention it, that's a splendid idea. But just to prove (a) that in *vino* there really is *veritas*, and (b) that I got more truth than wine out of those mortally wounded soldiers Morris left around, I shall give you a philosophical disquisition on my reactions to the evening's palaver."

"Disquish away," Madeleine said as she slid under him to the driver's side. "Nothing could be worse than it was."

Pietro settled back, held his left thumb, and ticked it with his right index finger. "Point number one. Though I hate to admit it, if a gun were put to my head I would have to say I find myself on the detestable Carlo's side: vegetarianism is precisely a culinary heresy.

"Having said that, however, I feel free to disagree with ninety percent of the substance of his remarks and a hundred percent of the style. Culinary theology is a subject for gentlemen—for people who can argue without impugning the moral character of their opponents. It is one thing to repel heresy; it is quite another to attempt to do so by being repulsive to heretics. Flies are caught with sugar; Carlo is one vast crock of vinegar.

"Point number two therefore: heresy cannot profitably be attacked by telling heretics they are wrong. To do so betrays a fatal ignorance of what heresy is. It is not an error; rather, it is a truth held in such isolation from other truths that it necessarily becomes only a half-truth. It is a violation, if you will, of the paradoxical largeness of reality."

"Excuse me," Madeleine interrupted, "but how do we get out of this dumb development?"

"Which one," Pietro asked, "the logical or the ontological?"

"The real estate-ological one, if Herr Professor can still remember his right from his left at this point."

"Left turns all the way till you get to the stop sign, then right. How's that for fast reflexes? Anything else? Or may I continue?"

"You may take three giant steps, for all I care. Just get to the point before we get home."

"I would have preferred umbrella steps," Pietro said; "but if you insist, I shall proceed straight on. Point number three is that the attractiveness of a heresy always proceeds more from the half of the truth it maintains than from the half of the truth it rejects. It is not, as the mindlessly orthodox often suppose, the things that heretics are against that put gas in their tanks; it's the things they are for. It's the goodness of veggies that keeps them going, not the badness of meat. Moreover, the good that they advocate is, as often as not, something the orthodox have neglected to pay sufficient attention to. Properly understood, heresy is almost always a reaction—albeit a lop-sided one—to a sad failure of catholicity on the part of those who claim to hold the wider truth.

"Witness, in the instant case, Carlo the Crass, a Defender, if there ever was one, whom the Faith could do without. Vegetables, in his book, amount to little more than the soggy potato that goes with his meat and, in August, the odd ear of foil-wrapped corn parched to death in charcoal. His defense of the orthodoxy of eating is about as welcome to a thinking person as a lecture on gardening from a man with an Astroturf lawn: he's disqualified himself on at least half the subject before he even starts."

"And you," Madeleine reminded him, "have used up three

LIGHT THEOLOGY & HEAVY CREAM

quarters of the trip home. You've got six blocks to get in the rest of the steps. Don't even bother to say, 'May I,' just head for the barn."

"As good as done," Pietro beamed. "Accordingly, since it is impossible to convince heretics of the error of their ways (for their ways, as far as they go, are good indeed), what is needed is a more conciliatory approach. The first step in any argument with vegetarians must be to sit with them and praise vegetables to the sky. They must feel themselves in the presence, not of enemies waiting for the chance to slap them to death with a steak, but of kindred souls who share their vegetable love.

"Only then may you proceed to hint at possible amendments of their ways—and even at that, you must not require them to move toward culinary orthodoxy one whit faster than their convictions will carry them. To illustrate, take the subject of beans. If your partners in dialogue are Total, or High Church vegetarians, you can never hope to gain their confidence by flaunting your (to them) latitudinarian love of beans drowned in butter. Instead, you get them to agree with you on the undesirability of merely watery string beans, and then invite them to consider the delights of beans in good olive oil—maybe, even with a few mushrooms and some almonds toasted in salt."

"One block," Madeleine called out. "Therefore . . . ?"

"Alas," sighed Pietro. "But if I must . . . Therefore: skipping over the various doctrines of beans as held by all the other sects of the vegetarian persuasion—by the Conservatives, or Ovo-lactarians; by the Broad Church, or Mrs.-Paul's-Fish-Stick Connexion; and by the Reformed, or Even-A-Little-Chicken-Soup Denomination—I conclude: since there isn't one of them that doesn't know something about beans, don't tell them they don't know beans about cooking. Instead, spill the bean recipes you know they can accept and . . ."

"Garage," Madeleine announced.

"How'd I do?" Pietro asked hopefully.

"I think," she said, "you're finally off your bean."

twenty-three

Ockham's Razor

There were twenty for dinner. The hostess took the leg of lamb out of the oven and stared at it. "Small? It's minuscule," she grumbled to her sister-in-law. "I knew I should have cooked two. The way Arthur carves, we'll be lucky if this serves eight."

Pietro propelled himself quietly away from the kitchen and took refuge in the living room under the lee of a stock market conversation. It was no use, though. She caught up with him just as they started in on horror stories about the latest mini-crash.

"I've come to rescue you from the bears and the bulls," she broke in airily. "Follow me." The lady was of that ripeness and perfectness of age at which women, even when they ask favors, act as if they are bestowing them.

"Your reputation is already made, of course, but just to keep it polished, I think you should carve for us." She put her lips to his ear and purred the confidential clincher. "I told Arthur a nine-pound leg was ridiculous. You're the only one here who can make it reach. Be a love."

Pietro wanted to tell her that carvers' reputations are

seldom improved on other people's roasts. More often they are shipwrecked between the Scylla of overcooked meat and the Charybdis of undersharpened knives. He said nothing, however. No man, having been aced into gallantry, and complaining about it, is fit to be listened to. He picked up the knife and checked the edge.

"I know it's not sharp," she admitted cheerfully, "but I'm sure you'll make do. There used to be one of those steel sharpening things around somewhere, but I think the children used it for a tent peg."

She flitted off, leaving Pietro to reflect on the over-confidence of the under-equipped. Had she asked him to drive railroad spikes with a cream puff, she could hardly have set him up worse. Still, if he did not like the position he was in, he'd been put there often enough to know the rules. The question in these press-gang carving sessions was not whether you could altogether keep from groaning "Alas!" as you worked. It was simply how long you could keep count of the total number of Alases.

He surveyed the roast. The odds against having to open with an Alas looked surprisingly good. The meat was not floating in a lake of its own wrung-out juices, and it still had a firm springiness to the touch. It was not, therefore, overdone. Lamb was the worst-cooked meat in America. Some culinary know-nothing had sold the entire country on 175 degrees as the correct internal temperature for a done leg. *Done-in* would have been a better word. What that prescription gave you was a haunch with a pot-roasted outside and a concrete center. The sharpest knife could do nothing but tear the surface meat to shreds, and the best gravy in the world couldn't disguise the dryness of the rest.

There was, of course, the unpleasant possibility that his hostess' roast might be stone-cold raw in the middle, but that was easy to check. Pietro stuck a carving fork into the thickest part of the meat, held it there for seven seconds, then whipped it out and touched a point to his lip. It was neither cool (which would have presaged a purple center), nor blistering (which would have foretold a vulcanized core), but just comfortably warm, promising a joint done exactly *au point* (140 degrees). The lady might not know from knives, but she did understand when to get a roast out of the oven. Pietro patted the leg approvingly and licked his fingers. By George! She had also managed to put a nicely herbed garlic crust on it. Things were looking up.

He had learned the hard way, though, not to rejoice too soon. He checked the upper end of the leg. Alas! Every bone with which the Creator had endowed the creature was still stubbornly in place: there could be no decent slices except from the very middle of the roast. Whatever happened to butchering in America? These supermarket lambs advertised as oven-ready were nothing of the sort. They received no loving preparation; they were simply stopped in their tracks and unceremoniously relieved of their hind quarters.

The time to work one's way around tail bone, backbone, aitch bone and shank, Pietro reflected, is before cooking, not after. And the culinary place for those bones is in the stock pot, where they can contribute to a good gravy, not in the roast, where they elicit nothing but a "good grief" from the carver. The living lamb may have enjoyed them in their original places, but now that we have so seriously disarranged his plans for the season, we ought not to balk at the relatively minor rearranging needed to make him fit in with ours.

Pietro sighed. There would be good slicing only in the middle; for the rest, it would be chipping and chunking all the way. He thought for a moment of boning out the best parts then and there and slicing them with better control on the cutting board. But Alas, there was no cutting board; and Alas, the knife was a ham slicer and had no point; and Alas, it was duller than dialectical materialism; and Alas . . .

Pietro caught himself. The purpose of checking out these dismal conditions was not to reduce him to whining but to send him forearmed to his work. He fetched an ovenproof platter from the dish closet and spent three minutes touching up the edge of the knife on the unglazed bottom ridge.

He allowed himself one last Alas. Who was it that led two hundred million people to forget that a knife has three parts: itself, its sharpening steel, and its cutting board? We do not expect scissors to work except in pairs, nor bridge games to be possible without a fourth. Why then do we expect one member of the carving trio to survive when the other two who sustain it are missing? The answer, he guessed, was that we don't, and that it doesn't—and that there was probably not one sharp knife to a suburb in all of America. For such a state our fathers fought and died?

Pietro turned the platter over and began carving. Finesse was out of the question; but then, he was asked only to make it do, not to make it thin. Anyway, he thought as he counted the slices onto a neat stack, people eat meat by number, not by size. A single piece of lamb, no matter how ample, seems not enough. Several smaller ones, served with a proper flourish, strike them as positively generous.

At twenty slices he stopped, cut the entire stack in three, arranged the results nicely on the platter and popped them into the warm oven.

"How many pieces did you get?" his hostess asked as she came back to dish up the potatoes.

"Sixty," he said. "Not counting the scraps we can still get off the bones."

"Wonderful," she murmured. "And you never even *thought* about complaining! I told you you were a love."

twenty-four

Dinner in the Diner

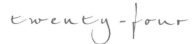

"Well!" Madeleine said to her sister as everybody piled into the car. "That was different. Who else besides Harry would take the world's fussiest cook to a *diner* for his birthday?"

Gina gave her husband a poke. "See? I told you it was a terrible idea. You have absolutely no class at all."

"I beg to differ." Pietro broke in soothingly from behind the wheel. "My respect for the tastes of my wife's brother-in-law is greater than ever. His dining instincts are strictly upper crust."

"Nonsense," Gina snapped from the rear seat. "The highest class I'll give him is lower middle. Look at the way he's got us riding, for heaven's sake: guys in the front, gals in the back. And as for that diner, it was hardly even redneck. I can't stand waitresses who call everybody 'Hon.'"

"Hey, Pete!" Harry grunted in his best redneck voice. "Whaddaya say we dump these two and replace 'em with a coupla nice Labradors? Be a lot quieter."

"You wish!" Gina shot back. "I still say it was a dumb idea."

"What's dumb?" Harry asked. "You got a terrific cook to treat, you don't take him to a terrific place. Chances are it still won't be as good as what he makes at home. Better you should give him something he'd never come up with in a million years."

"Well this certainly was *that*," Madeleine muttered. "But . . ."

Pietro cut her off. "No buts. He's got a lot stronger argument than you two victims of gourmet prejudice think. For one thing, the prices were fantastic. What was the tab, Harry?"

"Thirty-two dollars; drinks, tip and all. Where else can you beat eight dollars a head?"

"Still . . ." Gina broke in.

"No stills, either," Pietro said. "Be fair. The food was good. Salad bar, first rate: honest-to-God dressings, not mucilage— and some nice extra touches like marinated chick-peas and macaroni salad."

Madeleine turned to Gina. "Don't fight him on that one. He has a secret love affair with pasta and mayonnaise."

"That happens to be true," Pietro admitted. "But this particular macaroni salad was exceptional. Perfect balance: not dry, not runny, neither over- nor under-onioned. Take my word. I am the Calvin Trillin of salad bars."

"The potato salad was nice too," Harry added. "Sort of Italian. I never had that before."

"But this was supposed to be dinner," Gina objected, "not a plumbers' lunch."

"Your prejudices are showing again, my Dear," Pietro bantered. "Not to mention a certain lack of historical perspective. Great Victorian dinners always included plumbers' lunch food. It was called the Savory. After seventeen courses, they trotted out creamed eggs on toast, or something, to fill up the corners. If you'd taken your macaroni salad after the main course as I did, you'd have found it delightful."

"Yecch!" said the two back-seat passengers.

"False!" said the driver. "And false, all your other objections. The manicotti were fine—they were in fact cannelloni, made with homemade pasta. The tomato sauce needed only a bit more butter to smooth its rough edges. The flounder was superb . . ."

"The liver wasn't," Gina interrupted. "I thought it was going to be calf's."

"That was the think of an inexperienced thinker," Pietro said. "The liver was precisely as represented. At $3.50, with onions, bacon and fries, it had to be beef—and frozen besides. After all, the diner is in *business*, not love.

"Oh, all right," Madeleine put in peaceably. "So the food really was good. But you've got to give into us on the desserts. Those pies started at sickly sweet and worked their way down to appalling."

"Did they ever!" Gina agreed. "Where do they get the nerve to hang out an 'All Baking Done On Premises' sign?"

Pietro suddenly pulled over to the side of the road, stopped the car and turned dramatically to Gina. "They get their nerve legitimately, my Dear, and from a long and proud tradition. Those pies were no mere pastries; they were Diner Pies, the like of which is unproducible on any other premises in the universe. The recipes are jealously guarded family secrets written on the backs of old hectographed menus in dialect Polish or demotic Greek. In them alone is recorded the precise composition of the lemon filling that tastes more like Pledge than Pledge itself. Only on those yellowed sheets can be found the secret of the Mighty Meringue that stands up even under a flatiron. Nowhere but in those hidden formulas can be discovered the exact mixture of corn syrup, gypsum, Noxzema and Dixie Peach Pomade that produces cream topping with a center like rubber and a surface like case-hardened steel. But alas, neither you, nor

I, nor any outsider will ever be privy to such mysteries. Ours is not to know, but only to masticate and to marvel."

"Oh," said Gina.

"See?" said Harry.

"My, my," said Madeleine.

"And many happy returns of the day to you all," said Pietro, smiling as he swung the car back on the road.

twenty-five

Spirituality

"Will you *please* stop pacing up and down," Madeleine snapped; "I'm trying to meditate and you're jamming the room with nervous vibrations."

Pietro stopped and sat down. "Sorry," he said. "It's just that I have to write a piece about spirituality, and I can't think of a thing to say."

"That's because it's not your subject," Madeleine said bluntly. "Write about something else."

"What do you mean, it's not my subject?" Pietro shot back. "I'm a preacher, am I not? I should be able to come up with at least a couple of ideas."

"Not necessarily," she replied. "That's the trouble with preachers. They act as if a seminary education and an ordination service could make up for a fundamental lack of talent in a given area."

"So," Pietro huffed; "I have no talent for spirituality?"

"Of course you don't. You have a tin ear on the subject.

There's no more shame in that than there is in being color-blind, which you also are. The only thing you need to remember is not to go running around handing out free advice about either spiritual exercises or color schemes."

Pietro looked defeated anyway. "What am I supposed to do about this article, then?"

"The same thing you did about picking out new paint for the sanctuary: leave the subject up to other people who have some talent for it."

"Like you, I suppose?" he said archly.

"Of course, like me," she answered. "You know perfectly well I take to prayer and meditation like a singer to singing. It's just what I do—what I've done all my life, for that matter."

"Such humility!"

"Nonsense," she said. "I'm only stating a fact. Spirituality is one of the diverse gifts of the Spirit: God gives it to some and not to others. I deserve no more credit for having it than for being five-foot-seven instead of four-foot-two. All I'm saying is that if people want something way up on the spirituality shelf, they shouldn't send a mere tiny tot to fetch it."

"Are all those gifted with spirituality also the soul of kindness like yourself?"

Madeleine's patience suddenly ran out. "Oh, knock it off. You want me to give you some ideas, or don't you?"

"Well . . . , yes."

"Then shut up and listen." Madeleine marshaled her thoughts quickly and plunged in. "First, it *is* a gift. And since the Spirit hands out gifts as *she* wills, people get neither credit for having them nor blame for not having them. 1 Corinthians 12:8, 'To one is given by the Spirit the utterance of wisdom, and so on.' You know what that means? It means that there will probably be tons of people to whom the Spirit does *not* give wisdom, because she figures that, since the church is a body, those who have wisdom will exercise it for the benefit of all the fools who don't. The church doesn't need to have all its members to have the gift of sight. One or two eyes are quite enough, thank you; a seeing liver is unnecessary. Ditto with spirituality. Most of the church is not going to be red-hot at prayer, so those who are good at it do it for those who aren't."

Pietro broke in. "Then what's the point of all the books and sermons urging people to be more spiritual?"

"Sometimes no point, sometimes all the point in the world," Madeleine answered. "If they're beating everybody over the head to come up to the same level of spirituality, then they're pointless. But if they're simply urging people with varying gifts for spirituality to do the best they can, then they're fine. Spirituality is like dancing. It's one of the great activities of human nature: even if you can only stumble through it with two left feet, you'll be more human doing it than not."

"How come you make spirituality sound so unspiritual? According to you, it's just another merely human knack."

" 'Just another,' I won't give you," she rebutted. "It happens to be one of the best. But 'merely human knack' is okay: spirituality is not going to be the cause of anybody's salvation. Only Jesus is that. He died for us while we were still sinners; he didn't say he was going to wait until we got our meditation meters to read one hundred-plus. Spirituality is nice, even terrific. It's also holy, just and good—like the Law, and morality, and proper table manners—but God doesn't make it a sticking point when it comes to salvation."

"*That* I understand," Pietro said. "As a matter of fact, that's exactly what people object to most in my preaching."

"Well, at least you're listening," she said. "And the reason why he doesn't make it a sticking point is that there are just too many unspiritual types around. In addition to the business-as-usual klutzes like yourself, there are also the comatose, the catastrophically freaked-out, and all the little babies who don't even live long enough to say 'Mama'. If Jesus died and rose for

all of *them*, he'd just be welshing if he tacked on spiritual profi-
ciency as a universal requirement."

"I like that," Pietro said. "It's the first spiritual advice I've
had in years that didn't make me feel guilty."

"Good," Madeleine answered. "But just to keep yourself
humble, why don't you leave me to meditate in my kind of peace
and go write your kind of piece?"

"*You* should write it, you know."

Madeleine looked at him in disbelief. "And I thought you
were really listening. Look: *I* pray, *you* write. That's the way the
gift cookie crumbles. Go scribble me something that makes
sense and I'll meditate up a storm as my part of the job."

twenty-six

The Final Hampton

Pietro lay in bed listening to the debate between his head, which wanted to sleep, and his stomach, which was becoming strident. He and Madeleine had just gotten home from a movie in East Hampton, followed by pizza in Sag Harbor. Along with uncounted beers, he had ingested at least two slices each of sausage, anchovy, onion, and pepperoni. Bicarbonate of soda seemed like a good idea, but when he tried to get the message through to his legs, they weren't taking calls.

"Did you see that girl outside the pizza place?" Madeleine asked as she bounced under the covers.

Pietro felt the bed yaw like a sloop in bad weather. "Which girl?" he groaned.

"The one with the T-shirt that said, 'Sag Harbor, The Un-Hampton'. How come there's no Hampton without a modifier? Going from west to east, you've got Westhampton, Westhampton Beach, Hampton Bays, Southampton, Bridgehampton, and East Hampton. But just plain Hampton doesn't exist. At least in Jersey there really is an Orange. What is a Hampton, anyway?"

"Ham is home," Pietro mumbled, "Ton is town. Hampton, hometown . . . Hamlet, Hampshire . . . Hampstead . . . Hampton . . ." He fell asleep.

He dreamed he was driving eastward along the South Fork of Long Island in search of the Unqualified Hampton. Compounded versions of it were everywhere, but none of them quite measured up to the hopes they inspired. Strangely, too, all their names were different in his dream.

He came first to Prehampton and Prehampton Beach. Being a cook, he decided to ignore the commonest embodiments of Hamptonness: real estate brokerages every hundred yards, tennis courts galore, boutiques with puns for names, and mini-malls with more antique shops than antiques. He would conduct his search by culinary criteria only.

Prehampton Beach was full of clues. If it was any true guide to the reality it anticipated, the Ultimate Hampton would abound with stores that offered fancy produce, imported cheeses, exotic coffee beans, astronomically priced cookware, and Häagen-Dazs cones. It would also be endowed with pubs and vitamin stores in equal number—the latter, Pietro supposed, to build up what the former tore down. Above all, the parking arrangements would be diagonal—and on the main street, not tucked away in back lots.

He munched a strawberry the size of a lemon and totted up the virtues of Prehampton. Even though its very name confessed it was not the 10 he sought, it deserved at least a 7—maybe even an 8, if you gave it credit for humility. But the final Hampton still waited to be discovered, so he pressed on to the east.

Hampton Tries was the next town in which he parked (parallel to the curb, alas, and with nary a Cuisinart in sight). But if its Hamptonicity was less than obvious, it more than made up for it with Trying. Pubs were almost as numerous as real estate offices. There was a pork store. And the local deli had not only French cheeses and Colombian beans but, wonder of wonders,

the only "Chic Peas" Pietro had ever seen. He bought two
pounds on the spot. Even in the perfect Hampton, there might
be long queues for peas like that.

But then it was onward and outward again, across the Canal
and into the most fabled Hampton of all: Twohampton (or
Toohampton, as some insist). Pietro assumed that the first
spelling was based on the fact that no matter what specialty
stores other Hamptons might boast, here there would be two of
every kind. The alternative spelling was no doubt attributable
to the envy of less happier Hamptons—places that found themselves unwilling or unable to act on the principle that nothing
succeeds like excess.

Still, it was a Hampton to be reckoned with. It had more
pubkeepers than realtors, more delis even than pubs, De Cecco
pasta available around every corner, and triple crêmes practically rolling onto the streets. All this, Pietro marveled, and diagonal parking too? Could this be the goal of his quest?

Sadly, he knew it could not. Excessive though it might be,
it only whetted the mind's appetite for profounder excess still.
The true Hampton Hunger could not rest even here. Unless
the world itself was a cruel joke, Pietro concluded, the grand
object of his desire—that Last Resort to which all Hamptons
point—must exist somewhere beyond. He drove eastward again.

Tokenhampton took him by surprise. He had assumed that
the stages of his pilgrimage would be an upward progress. But
here he had come to a halt in something that could only be described as a Prehampton Beach without diagonal parking or, less
kindly, as a Hampton Tries with new paint and Cuisinarts. Perhaps, Pietro thought, Toohampton had jaded rather than sharp-
ened his tastes. After all, Tokenhampton had coffee beans,
cookware, cheeses and pubs. But try as he might to be fair, it was
plainly not the perfection he sought. He had no choice but to
move on in the hope that the last Hampton known to man
would somehow be the Hampton of his heart.

The minute he entered Fartoohampton, he knew he was doomed to disappointment. The all-important note of excess was present, to be sure. But what good was even freshly painted excess, Pietro thought, without diagonal parking? It was just Bloomingdale's in the boondocks. Besides, the excess of Fartoohampton was of a particularly perilous sort.

Admittedly, no Hampton of any kind could exist without the luxuries that only Manhattan could provide. But in New York, the extravagances of the City's heart were counterbalanced by the sheer weight of the metropolitan area. If there was *Lutece*, there was also Blimpie's. If there was Bendel's, there was also the brash young man at 34th and 7th with a cardboard box of blouses. Dumas' pastries were kept humble by the citywide presence of pistol-holster turnovers; the Bridge Company's copper *sautoirs* by cheap aluminum pots in a thousand hardware stores.

But when such extravagance was plunked down next to a sand dune, it gave off an air, not of humility but of hybris. No, however much Pietro might have hoped that Fartoohampton would embody the Hamptonality yet to come, it too fell short of the glory. The longed-for Hampton would have to come side by side with a New York to which it was inseparably joined, but from which it could remain forever distinct.

Pietro sighed, started his car and once more took the highway east. His mind expected nothing more, but his heart was still drawn. He drove entranced through the last outposts of the world—Amagansett, Napeague, Hither Hills, Ditch Plain—to the Very Point itself. And there, in the blaze of the noonday sun, his eyes finally saw the eschatological Hampton descending in glory. Celestial Manhattan followed in its train. Archangels rained down *pâtés* upon the earth, pizzas with white truffles fell like manna from heaven, and choirs of angels sang

"Blessed City, heavenly Hampton,
Vision dear of specialties . . ."

Pietro leaped from his car, threw his credit cards to the wind and raced to greet the vision . . .

He woke up in a heap on the bedroom floor.

"Are you all right?" Madeleine asked, switching on the light. "I've heard you sing in your sleep before, but this is the first time you ever dove out of bed. What happened?"

He rubbed himself groggily. "Comes from eating pizza in an Un-Hampton, I guess. I'll tell you about it in the morning. Where's the bicarb?"

COWLEY PUBLICATIONS is a ministry of the brothers of the Society of Saint John the Evangelist, a monastic order in the Episcopal Church. Our mission is to provide books and resources for those seeking spiritual and theological formation. COWLEY PUBLICATIONS is committed to developing a new generation of writers and teachers who will encourage people to think and pray in new ways about spirituality, reconciliation, and the future.